How to Make Friends That Last

A Comprehensive Guide to Meeting New People and Making Friends - Self-Help Book for Meaningful Connections and Long-Lasting Bonds

Adults and Teens

Paul Richter

Contents

INTRODUCTION

In our fast-paced, isolated world, it's easy to feel like we're the only ones struggling to make friends. Everyone else seems to have a thriving social life, while we're stuck at home with our Netflix account and a pint of ice cream. But the truth is, making friends can be challenging for everyone—even those who seem to have it all together. It's not impossible to build meaningful relationships, though. With a little effort and courage, you can develop lasting friendships that will enrich your life in ways you never thought possible. This book will show you how to take the first steps toward building a social life that works for you.

Are you a teen or adult with a strong desire to make lasting friendships but lack the social skills or confidence to do so?

Perhaps you need help making friends due to various circumstances, such as divorce, remote work, or moving to a new city. Or do you often feel shy or anxious in social situations, making it difficult to meet new people and form close bonds?

Another crucial factor is that we often face internal obstacles that hinder our social skills, such as social anxiety, fear of rejection, or a lack of confidence.

However, while it may be challenging to create and maintain friendships, there are many ways that we can work on improving our social skills, and this book is here to help you overcome these challenges so that you may create lasting friendships.

This book is excellent for people of all ages who want to improve their friendship skills. It guides you through the process of making friends, from meeting people and forming connections to knowing when to let go of unhealthy friendships. That is if you're looking for a book to help you build confidence and find true friends.

Inside *How to Make Friends That Last,* you will...

- learn how to make friends as an adult.

- develop the skills necessary to create close, lasting friendships.
- overcome obstacles that have been preventing them from making friends.
- gain confidence in social situations.
- achieve long-lasting, meaningful friendships.

Who is the esteemed author, you may ask? Paul Richter.

When we love, we always strive to become better than we are. When we strive to become better than we are, everything around us becomes better too… –Paulo Coehlo

He was born and raised in Leipzig, Germany, and attended the University of West London, where he attained a degree in Nursing. He currently works as a Primary Care Manager with a background in cardiothoracic intensive care.

As someone who has moved to a different country, Paul is all too aware of the challenges some people find when making new friends and building self-confidence—overcoming the struggles they face when meeting someone for the first time in a given situation. It also explores many common misconceptions and limiting beliefs surrounding the idea of making friends and provides valuable solutions for overcoming them.

Today, Paul lives in London with his pet Dalmatian. In his spare time, he enjoys hiking, writing, baking French macarons, reading, running with his dog, and going to the cinema.

He also devotes some of his time to volunteering at a local shelter, and when he has the chance, he likes to travel and immerse himself in the food, wine, and culture of new places.

Paul's hopes for the future include using his writing as a vehicle that will enable him to become a digital nomad, travel to far-flung places, work with medical missions, and help the less fortunate in the poorer communities of the world.

In today's world, it's easy to get caught up in our own lives and forget the importance of friendships. But as this book will show, friendships are crucial at any age, and it's never too late to learn the skills to make new, lasting friendships.

Making friends as an adult can be difficult, but it is possible if you know how. Everyone has the ability to overcome their obstacles and build their confidence to make meaningful friendships that will inevitably enrich their lives. Yes, that means you too.

Say goodbye to awkward silences, having conversations in "interview mode," struggling to hold someone's attention, your lack of self-awareness, and limiting beliefs.

This guide is filled with advice that is backed by science, learned through years of experience, and made practical so that you can learn to open up to people easily, tell captivating stories, have confidence and charisma, make good initial impressions, keep the conversation flowing and smooth, ask better questions, and go deep in a warm way.

Making new and lasting friendships has never been this straightforward.

What are you waiting for?

CHAPTER 1:

WHY MAKING FRIENDS IS SO IMPORTANT

We all know how important it is to have friends when we're younger. But what about when we're adults? And why is making friends so important? There are lots of benefits to adult friendships. For one, friends can provide a sense of security. They can help us feel less anxious and stressed and even improve our moods. Plus, friendships can be a great source of support during tough times. This chapter will examine why friendships are meaningful, how they can help us grow, and common misconceptions about making new friends.

How Important Is Friendship in Your Life?

Our connections evolve as we get older. Finding a life partner and preserving family connections take up a lot of attention in adulthood, so our friendships can suffer if they take a back seat. Because we all have limited time, it can be challenging to prioritize friends among the responsibilities of a job, home, and family. However, adulthood does not change the significance of friendship!

Friendship is a unique type of relationship. Friends serve as cheerleaders, confidants, support networks, and more. It's powerful to share your past with someone. After being friends for a while, you begin to understand each other better. You'll have inside jokes and recollections to share. When you can share life's blessings with someone you genuinely care about, those blessings create an even greater sense of fulfillment.

Why Should Adults Have Friends?

You need more than one connection to satisfy all your needs. Since we are all humans, we were created for interpersonal interaction. It's almost impossible for one person to be everything you need all the time. It's selfish to expect someone like our spouse to meet all our wants and needs. Often, they won't have the same energy, schedule, or frame of mind as us. Your spouse might need time to read their new books while you crave an outdoor outing. Even though you adore each other, it's challenging to be constantly surrounded by the same person. You may address diverse demands by spending time with a range of individuals. You could, for instance, have friends who encourage your creativity and others who provide you with sound counsel when you need a shoulder. Friendships may be used for a variety of things.

Even the concept of friendship may vary from one relationship to the next. Some friendships are founded on convenience or closeness. Consider your interactions with colleagues or neighbors. Even if it's only to ask someone to bring in the mail while you're out of town, it's always nice to have friends you can rely on.

Some friendships may be more intimate, especially those founded on a shared passion or activity. These relationships may give you a feeling of belonging and open doors for meeting new individuals.

The "best friends" form of friendship is with those that are close. Deep, profound ties are made between close friends.

As you can see, creating long-lasting friendships has many purposes and benefits; let's look at more benefits.

The Benefits of Friendships

A true friend won't only look to you for assistance; authentic friendships also require mutual support and respect. They'll be there for you when they can, whether with words of encouragement or simply by listening.

The icing on the cake is that a healthy friendship also benefits your health!

Friendship Offers Support

Friends are often each other's most significant sources of support. Friendship provides you with someone to trust, share knowledge with, laugh with, seek counsel from, or turn to for emotional support. Friends are particularly crucial for those who don't have close ties to their family. When life becomes challenging, friends support us. They provide us with guidance, solace, and emotional security.

Encouragement When Times Are Tough

Life can become challenging at certain times.

You could encounter distressing or challenging situations that impact your emotional well-being at any moment and without notice, such as...

- separation or divorce.
- death of a loved one or pet.
- illnesses.
- unemployment.
- relationship troubles.

Any of these difficulties can significantly impact long-term mental health results. However, according to a 2017 study, having close friends would probably make it simpler to deal with whatever challenges life presents (Raypole, 2020). It's conceivable that friendship will be especially useful for coping with the stress brought on by familial issues, such as abuse and neglect.

Friends Give Us a Sense of Belonging

Our sense of belonging is increased through friendships. It feels nice when others welcome us—the struggle of solitude. Because we're not made for it, loneliness may adversely affect our physical and emotional health. It's important to spend time with people who love and accept you for who you are. Everyone has concerns; therefore, having friends who embrace us despite those concerns is necessary.

Everybody wants to feel important and that their life has meaning. In reality, safety requirements and basic needs (such as food and shelter) come before belonging needs in Maslow's hierarchy of needs.

Life is more meaningful when you care about other people. When you care for someone else, you accept the obligation to show compassion and provide emotional support. You may become a more resilient and admirable person as a result.

Friends May Increase Self-Confidence

Being taken care of by someone is comforting. It might be reassuring to know that someone is on your side. Your friends may serve as a reminder of all your strengths. You might feel more confident when you see what your friends find admirable in you. Imagine what your close friends might say to you, even if you don't feel particularly confident in yourself. How might they motivate you? They'll likely shower you with kind words about all your greatest accomplishments!

Having Friends to Talk to Can Reduce Anxiety Levels

Everybody experiences stress. Whether it comes in large or small quantities, it may overwhelm you, no matter how insignificant it may appear. Stress may cause you to experience mood symptoms like anxiety, despair, or irritability.

Long-term stress can lead to...

- inadequate immune system.
- insomnia.
- digestion issues.
- heart complications.
- high blood pressure.
- diabetes.

However, there is some good news! According to research, keeping close connections can increase your ability to manage stress and decrease your likelihood of experiencing various forms of stress (Raypole, 2020).

Remember the last time anything caused you to get agitated or anxious. It's possible that you confided in a friend about your problems; they listened to your rant and helped you come up with constructive solutions. The ability to count on the support of friends and family can help reduce the effects of several stressors before they become overwhelming.

Friendships Enrich Our Lives

Friendships improve our lives by supporting, welcoming, and boosting our self-esteem. When we need encouragement, friends can drive us to do our best. Even mundane activities may take on new significance with loved ones by our side. Friendship is a two-way connection that requires both parties to function. All these advantages are not only for you but also for your friends. That's quite fantastic!

Here is a summary and a few more reasons why friendships are so meaningful at any stage of our lives:

- People are social creatures and need friends for support.
- Adult friendships can provide a sense of community and connection often missing in our lives.
- Friends can help us learn more about ourselves and grow as individuals.
- They can make us feel happier and more fulfilled.
- They can help us stay connected to our passions and interests.
- They can introduce us to new people and experiences.
- They are a great way to build relationships with more like-minded people.
- They can help keep us mentally healthy.
- Friendships bring happiness and fulfillment into our lives.

Now that you know how beneficial it is to have good friends in your life, when is the perfect time to make new friends? Right now!

Why Is Now the Perfect Time to Make New Friends?

We discussed the importance of friendship, why we need friends as adults, and how having true friends can benefit our mental, physical, and emotional well-being. Having someone to share the significant and not-so-significant moments in life with is something we all crave. But how do you know if you're ready to make new friends?

If you're wondering if it's time for a new friendship, look at "why" it is:

- You're more settled in your life and know what you want.
- It's easier than ever to meet new people with the internet and social media.
- You're more open-minded and tolerant now than when you were younger.
- Making friends is a great way to boost your mental health and well-being.
- Friends can introduce you to new experiences, activities, and opportunities.
- Friendship is a two-way street: you can offer support and companionship to your friends too.
- There are now more online and in-person meetups available than ever before.
- It's always possible to make new friends.

So, you're all fired up and ready to jump in and make new friends! But you have some hesitations... If your hesitations have anything to do with the following list of myths, then you're all good to go!

Myths About Making Friends

Our ideas about friendship are often simplistic. We often use clichés like "best friends forever" to talk about friendships while ignoring the complexity of these important bonds. Despite its simplicity, misconceptions have developed. The following few friendship misconceptions need to be dispelled:

- **Friendships are meant to endure a lifetime, and that's how it should be**. However, most people keep different friends throughout their lives. People evolve, as do their environments and the qualities they value in friends. The idea that friendships frequently end and fizzle out is okay! It happens.
- **True friends never have conflict. Just as in every relationship, conflict is good and common among friend-**

ships. Friendship is the interplay of two complicated, constantly evolving human beings. You occasionally disagree, but that doesn't mean you're not still friends. Friendships frequently become stronger if you can resolve conflicts openly and sincerely.

- **There is no rekindling of a friendship after it has faded**. Although some friendships do end for good, others rekindle after a break or an especially trying time. It's possible that old friends drifted apart in college and reconnected as adults. A friend going through a trying time could withdraw and reappear once they've dealt with their issues. People who had drifted apart in the past may come back together due to a significant event or the co-occurrence of a life stage (such as having kids). There is no one path to friendship and intimacy.
- **Friends will naturally understand your needs; if they don't, they aren't good friends**. You can't expect your friends to read your mind! One friend must express their feelings when hurt, while the other needs some space. It is impossible to expect a friend—even one you've known for 20 years—to understand your needs without your help. We need to express verbally what we need and when.
- **If a friendship ends, it means you've failed**. By all means, grieve about a friendship that is gone. But sometimes, it's okay to call it quits on a friendship, demonstrating maturity. The healthiest course of action may be to leave a friendship when it no longer seems mutual, when it feels one-sided, when there is no longer a connection, or when different needs and worldviews are encountered.
- **There is only one kind of perfect friendship**. There are many distinct kinds of friendships. Some people start when they are young and never stop being friends. Other friendships remain in summer camp. While some friendships are close-knit, others are primarily in the same social circles we find ourselves. We could discover that we favor particular individuals for friendship in specific scenarios. Others simply prefer only close-knit or only casual relationships. There

is no one-size-fits-all approach to keeping friendships alive; whatever works for you is all that matters.

Here are a few more myths you should dismiss:

- You must be super outgoing to make friends.
- All your friends need to like the same things that you do.
- Making friends is impossible if you move to a new city or country.
- You can only make friends if you go out and socialize a lot.
- You can't be too picky about who your friends are.
- It's hard to make friends once you're an adult.
- It's easier to make friends when you're younger.
- Introverts and shy people don't stand a chance.

What exactly is wrong with these myths? They are generalizations. If we believe them, it will be impossible to make friends! We need to question our assumptions about friendship, dispel myths and prejudices, and create the connections that are most beneficial to us.

The idea of making a group of new friends sounds fantastic, and your weekends will ultimately be filled with many memorable adventures! But we all know that friendship does not just happen overnight and that it's much easier said than done. The following chapter will discuss why it might be harder to make friends as we get older and what could be holding us back from forming close relationships with other individuals.

CHAPTER 2:

THE CHALLENGE OF MAKING FRIENDS AS AN ADULT

We all have different comfort levels when meeting new people and making friends. For some of us, starting a conversation with a stranger and making a new friend is effortless. We're outgoing and confident, and we enjoy being surrounded by people. Others of us are more introverted and find social situations more daunting. We're not necessarily shy but prefer smaller groups or one-on-one interactions. And then there are those of us who fall somewhere in between. No matter where you fall on the spectrum, it's essential to be comfortable with yourself and your ability to make new friends.

After all, friendships are essential to our lives, providing us with support, companionship, and a sense of belonging. Do you feel like you're struggling to make friends? You're not alone. Millions of people feel the same way. But that doesn't mean you can't overcome your struggles and build lasting friendships.

Why Is Making Friends as an Adult More Challenging?

We're more tolerant and curious as children. As adults, we've developed a set of standards to evaluate others. Unfortunately, we become selective about the types of friends we want. This restricts our connections because we ignore those who could give us unique perspectives and experiences.

Making friends as an adult is not impossible, but it feels like it. It takes patience to persevere through unpleasant experiences. We find it awkward or too time-consuming to pursue a new connection because we're either too shy or afraid of rejection. Your mind races with unpleasant thoughts before you even dare to say hello.

What if I don't know what to say?

Do they even want a new friend?

Will they genuinely like me for who I am?

Our current social structure is very unlike how humans naturally survive and function. As the structure of society goes, we tend to place a high value on individualism, making it challenging for an adult to make friends.

Once you leave school, where everyone serves their time and shares a shared experience for years, you're on your own. The circumstances for creating genuine friendships are rare unless you make it your purpose to create them. Everyone is at a loss for what to do, and you are now alone and responsible for your destiny. There is no clear path forward at this point. You are free to live the life you wish.

You may decide to avoid making new friends and give up the pursuit. But the truth is, we need to endure that sometimes awkward phase of first getting to know someone before we realize how valuable that friendship has become over the time you've spent together and how much this person, who was once a stranger, has become part of your life and changed it for the better.

You can create genuine friendships if you maintain your patience and easygoing approach from when you were just a kid. Become curious as to what people do in their free time. Does it match up with your interests or hobbies? You will never know unless you get out there and start a conversation.

Do not let fear, your schedule, preconceived notions, or comfort keep you from creating connections.

Here is a summary of why we struggle to build meaningful relationships as adults:

- Adults are busy. We have less time to socialize than when we were younger.
- It's harder to make friends as adults because we are more guarded and selective about who we let into our lives.
- It's easier to stay connected with friends from childhood or college than to make new ones.
- We move away from our hometowns or change jobs, making it difficult to maintain relationships.
- Technology has made it easier for people to isolate themselves from others.
- The way friendships are formed has changed over the years, making it more difficult to build lasting connections.

We are constantly seeking new methods to expand our networks, strengthen our bonds, and establish the sense of belonging that is most encouraging to us. But first, let's take a look back and get some perspective through self-reflection.

Self-Reflection Questions

Personal introspection is essential. When we look back, we need to consider all our blessings, contemplate what was important to us in the past, and question whether it still is. It's a way for you to feel proud of my accomplishments and pay respect to the setbacks and defeats. Taking an identity snapshot helps us be more mindful of our future objectives. It gives us a better understanding of where we've come from. It's equally crucial that we consider why some friendships worked so well and others did not, so we may learn from our past mistakes.

Here are some self-reflection questions to consider before making new friends:

- Why do you want more friends?
- Do you struggle to make or keep friends? What do you think is the reason?
- Are you too guarded and protective of your personal life?
- What is at the root of anxiety in social settings?
- Have you been hurt in the past and are scared to open up again?
- Do you spend too much time on social media staying connected with old friends, not making space for new ones?

As you become honest and open during your reflection, you might notice a pattern emerge. Have you been avoiding new connections because you were too afraid to open up to someone because you were let down in the past? Perhaps you had a really good friend and thought the world of them. Still, their actions disappointed you somewhere along the line. You felt like you no longer had that strong connection because of how things unfolded. Whatever the case, we need to explore what might be holding you back from making lasting friendships.

What's Holding You Back?

You are not alone if you experience loneliness or feel as though you have no friends. While it may seem unattainable or challenging to meet new people as an adult, you can develop new connections if you're prepared to put in the time and effort.

In this section, we'll discuss why it may be hard for you to establish friendships and the psychological effects of isolation.

What Could Be Holding You Back

It is usual for people to feel like they do not have enough friends. Many people experience loneliness or believe that others cannot relate to them. There are several reasons we might feel something is holding us back from connecting with others.

Here is a list of reasons you might feel that way:

Anxiety

The fact that so many individuals get nervous when they meet new people is a frequent reason for this. The source of this anxiety is a worry about being disapproved of or criticized by others.

Concentrating on the other person and maintaining eye contact when feeling anxious or unsure of ourselves is hard. This prevents us from connecting with others. And then, we start avoiding establishing acquaintances due to these unpleasant feelings.

Examine your thoughts and emotions the next time you make an effort to make friends to see whether you have any anxiety, worry, or nervousness. Then consider if these sensations or ideas promote or prevent your ability to create friends. By doing this, you can learn whether this is a reason why you struggle to develop lasting friendships.

Avoidance

Do you ever shy away from or decline opportunities because you don't want to deal with the challenges of establishing friendships? Our tendency to avoid difficult situations might sometimes go undetected or ignored.

Therefore, consider your reasons when you decline social invitations. Be aware of that choice and the reason behind it. When you don't consciously try to meet new people, it will be tough for you to develop any new connections!

High Standards

The need to be well-liked and well-connected is a common source of stress for many individuals. It is not necessary to have a large group of friends; occasionally, having only one or two will be enough to reap the rewards of strong connections on a psychological level. Put less emphasis on making a large number of friends and instead concentrate on developing one or two significant relationships.

When contemplating what might hold you back, you must consider the growing list of obstacles contributing to this dilemma.

The obstacles you might face are...

- fear of approaching people you don't know.
- developing trust and friendship.
- maintaining relationships over time.
- that you don't know where to meet new people.
- that it's hard for you to make small talk.
- that you're too busy with work and other obligations.
- that you're shy or introverted.

There is a never-ending list of obstacles or reasons why we cannot make new connections effectively, but that doesn't mean we're a lost cause. It means there are things we might need to work on within ourselves before we can confidently approach others and form a bond.

Let's take a deeper look into why we're struggling with this seemingly easy task of making new friends.

Diving Deeper

There are a lot of possible explanations for why you don't have many friends (or any). These reasons are, of course, unique to each person.

Let's look at some common reasons you may not have friends:

- **You have a shy personality**. Some people find it difficult to strike up a conversation with strangers. You fear going out in public and prefer to spend time alone at home rather than interacting with others.
- **You struggle with social anxiety**. The experience of extreme dread in social circumstances is known as social anxiety. It can paralyze you to the point that you can't do the things that could bring you joy, like reaching out to others and establishing new relationships.
- **You're permanently relocating**. Making and keeping friends might be difficult if you travel around a lot. You might need to start over after you become used to a new group of close friends.
- **You are an outcast**. Maybe you just like being alone yourself. Some individuals, particularly introverts, believe they ought to have more companions yet actually enjoy their alone time.
- **Your interests are different from those of your coworkers and neighbors**. You might prefer drinking tea and going to coffee shops to drinking beer and watching football.
- **You have no idea where to start looking.** Your profession or lifestyle may limit your chances of meeting people in person, and you may not know where to look.
- **You're trying much too hard**. You may be trying too hard to establish friendships, which backfires when people interpret you as needy or lead you to reveal too much about yourself too quickly.
- **Your friendships are not a top priority**. Although you may have a few friends or acquaintances, you don't stay in touch with them, and soon they stop getting in touch with you.

- **Your relationships with others are only fleeting**. Although you are well acquainted with many individuals, you keep your distance from them.
- **You already have a "full" life**. Perhaps you're preoccupied with a demanding job, family responsibilities, education, or other commitments.

The list can go on forever! To truly understand why we struggle to make meaningful connections, we need to reflect on our thoughts, feelings, and nature. We'll discover that the main reason we can't make friends is that, in some way or another, we're holding ourselves back, sometimes without even realizing it.

Here is a summary of potential deeper reasons why you might struggle to make connections:

- Lack of confidence.
- Lack of initiative.
- Feelings of awkwardness.
- Social anxiety.
- Shyness or Introversion.
- Low self-esteem.
- Fear of rejection.

This information might feel overwhelming, but I have good news. You can overcome the challenges you face. No matter what they are or how many of them you struggle with. If you genuinely wish to make a change and are willing to put in the effort required to make that change, then anything is possible.

CHAPTER 3:

OVERCOMING YOUR CHALLENGES

No one ever said that making friends would be easy. It comes naturally for some people, while the rest struggle to find common ground with others. If you're struggling to make friends, don't worry—you're not alone. But thankfully, there are steps that you can take to overcome your challenges and start building relationships with others.

What Does It Take To Make New Friends as an Adult?

Meeting prospective friends in person requires putting yourself in a vulnerable position compared to simpleminded online interactions. You may carefully construct your messages or quickly close a tab when you need a break. But in reality, things are more complex.

We all experience initial awkwardness or uncomfortable feelings as we approach someone new. Our nerves go haywire as we try to find the right things to say without making them sound too rehearsed. But when someone approaches us, we are thrilled to accept a new invitation to get to know this person better. We need to be that person from now on! You can't always expect others to initiate the conversation; you need to become more vulnerable and put yourself out there.

There are many chances to meet new people face to face; you simply need to keep your eyes open and know what to do when you spot a potential friendship.

A summary of what this chapter will discuss is the following:

- Evaluate what you're looking for in a friend (this is important! We'll discuss some desirable traits later on).
- Identify your social circles and assess whether they offer potential friends (at the gym, at work, perhaps on your commute?).
- Get involved in activities and groups that interest you (hello, book club!).
- Reach out to people you already know, even if you don't consider them friends yet (again, this can be at work, your next-door neighbor, or that nice person at church).

- Be open to new experiences and meet new people (try something new every once in a while).
- Don't be afraid to put yourself out there (Yes, this is necessary)!

Here, friendship specialists offer their best guidance on how to meet people and form new friendships as an adult (Yankovich, 2022):

Find a Means to Connect With Others Who Have Similar Hobbies or Interests

Even if joining a book club, sports team, or other recreational group sounds like cliché advice, there's a good reason for it.

Making friends involves two primary steps:

1. Introducing yourself to others.
2. Discovering those interested in connecting with you.

People who participate in group hobbies almost always do so for social and recreational reasons.

To put it another way, being a part of a community of individuals who share your interests and goals will increase your chances of meeting someone who shares your interests and goals.

These groups also offer a key to friendship-building; frequent exposure to one another.

You might consider participating in a recurring activity to meet new people and form lasting friendships. This will allow you to take advantage of the "mere exposure effect," the unconscious propensity to like individuals we've spent time with before. By partaking in a regular activity, you build a network and reduce your need to constantly make new acquaintances while still getting frequent exposure to them.

Suppose you don't make your "best friend" at your group's first or second meeting. In that case, the simple exposure hypothesis is another compelling argument to keep trying. As you know, it takes time to develop a friendship. Therefore, the more frequently you turn up, the more probable you may meet someone in the following weeks or months.

Put Your Phone Away!

Whether you're glued to your phone at a backyard barbecue or killing time by scrolling your thumbs off while waiting for your boxing class to start, there's no disputing that technology may hinder our capacity to meet new people.

Suppose I'm looking around for someone friendly, and I notice that they seem uninterested or too busy to talk. In that case, I will not waste my time attempting to strike up a conversation with them. You convey that you are not interested in interacting with others when you scroll on your phone. Make sure your body language conveys how ready you are to start a discussion (yes, it's necessary to smile and uncross your arms too).

When Meeting New Individuals, Always Be Positive

Keeping an eye on your tone when others are around is also a good idea. If you're grumbling about how you'd rather be at home or that the place you're in might need some work, that will make it challenging for someone to approach you.

Similarly, try not to start a conversation on a sour note. You could accidentally put a damper on a growing friendship. Instead, try opening up discussions with compliments such as "that picture is fantastic" or "the starters are all delicious tonight."

Use your "positive" comment as a conversation starter by following it up with a question directed toward the individual, such as "What type of art are you into?" or "What is your favorite starter so far?" These are great follow-up questions to learn more about the person you're talking to.

A study from Harvard (Tamir & Mitchell, 2012) discovered that self-disclosure stimulates brain areas linked with pleasure, providing further evidence that people like the possibility of talking about themselves. Therefore, a proven approach to starting a discussion on a good note is to offer a polite yet personal question.

How You Leave a Discussion Is Just as Significant as How You Enter It

Few things are more frustrating than leaving a fantastic conversation with someone and not knowing if you'll ever see them again. Making new friends requires starting and participating in discussions, but how you conclude those encounters may be equally important.

But how can one keep the fun going? Pay close attention to the ebb and flow of your talk so that you might plant a seed when you part ways. You might say, "I know a few hiking areas that you would love," to wrap up a conversation with someone who says they want to go hiking that week. "Do you use Instagram? I'm going to share a link with you!" After your initial engagement, the objective is to consciously establish a space where you can stay in touch, either in person or online.

Strike up a One-On-One With a New Friend You Made During an Event

You may have met this person at a knitting group or hiking club, and now you see them frequently. What's next? The ideal approach to advancing your friendship is through a one-on-one activity. When you meet someone you like, consider creating exclusivity by having experiences with them that you don't have with the other group members.

Making this development is a crucial relationship milestone since it is one of the simplest ways to develop the intimacy that fosters friendship. It may be suggested that you grab a quick meal after an exercise class, take a lunchtime stroll around the block, or get ready for an event you're both attending. Suppose you are hesitant to approach them on a one-on-one basis. In that case, you may invite them to a social activity you are arranging (such as a birthday celebration or picnicking at the park).

Take Steps to Cultivate and Strengthen Your Professional Friendships

There's a good possibility you've had a work friend if you've ever worked closely with your coworkers, whether at desks next to each other, in a kitchen, or behind a service counter. One of the most common places where people establish acquaintances is at their workplace.

Friendships formed at work often extend into the outside world. Yet, it's essential to respect the personal space of both coworkers and superiors. Changing the environment may do wonders for the chemistry of a relationship that began in the workplace.

It will be challenging to maintain a friendship with someone you only engage with at work after you leave your current place of employment. The best way to get to know someone is to spend time with them in various environments since this will allow you to see who they are. For instance, a coworker could feel much more at ease opening up about their private life while getting ice cream or attending a sporting event together as opposed to when they're in the communal kitchen area of the workplace.

If you want to become friends with a coworker but are still deciding whether to take your relationship outside of the office, talking about things other than work is a fantastic way to measure how comfortable you are with one another. You can connect through music by sharing a playlist you've enjoyed lately or by recommending a new restaurant. The goal is to show a more complex side of yourself, so you can determine whether there is a chance for a lifelong, real-world friendship.

Let Them Know Right Away if You Two Click

Like in a romantic relationship, it's essential to express your feelings for a new acquaintance and find out whether they feel the same way about you. Unsurprisingly, research demonstrates that we have the propensity to like those who like us.

To oversimplify, sometimes you must let someone know (in a lighthearted way) that you appreciate them. You'll direct your intentions by expressing your enjoyment of their company or your opinion of them as fun and fascinating.

Research from 2018 indicated that people frequently underrate how much others appreciate and enjoy their presence. Making your feelings clear to a possible friend helps progress your connection with them, especially if you share the trait of leaving conversations uncertain as to where you stand with people and want to be liked. In this way, you will have a clear understanding of whether or not the feeling is mutual.

Our Sense of Self

We need to take a deeper look at how our behavior might influence our connections with others. We are often quick to judge others and nitpick on what traits we want in a friend, but do we have those traits we desire in others?

The following are some traits that you might need to work on yourself:

- **Openness**: Have a curious mind and a desire for new experiences.
- **Agreeableness**: Have a good nature and be willing to help people. How can you offer your assistance?
- **Consciousness:** Be dependable and accountable. Do you deliver on your promises?
- **Self-Awareness**: If you have a strong sense of self-awareness, then you are confident in who you are and accept yourself wholeheartedly. If others see how comfortable you are, they will most likely unwind and be more open.
- **Self-Reflection**: Know who you are and what you like! Suppose you know what hobbies and activities you enjoy. In that case, you will most likely meet like-minded individuals in those spheres and make lifelong connections.
- **Open-Mindedness**: Be more open to new experiences and people; be willing to try new things.
- **Friendly**: When meeting new individuals, be optimistic!

- **Persistence**: Friendships take a long time to develop, and they are persistent in making meaningful connections. Don't be discouraged by the amount of time and effort required to make it work!
- **Social Skills**: When we improve our social skills, we find connecting and interacting easier.

Use the list above as a guideline to shift your way of thinking and the way you approach friendship. If you find that you need to be more friendly or that you might not be as open to new experiences, then try to work on those traits. Offer a simple hello and a friendly smile to a stranger as you pass them by on the street or the next time an opportunity arises that sounds like fun. Still, if you feel hesitant at first, give it a go! You can practice and define your traits when meeting someone new and in everyday situations.

Are you feeling a little overwhelmed? That's okay! As you put your new knowledge into practice, you'll see that once you overcome the initial fear of getting to know someone and put in the effort to remain consistent in your promises and actions (and they do too), you'll soon find yourself in a positive and blossoming friendship.

CHAPTER 4:

BUILDING SELF-CONFIDENCE

Do you feel shy or uncomfortable in social situations? Maybe you're afraid to talk to new people or don't know how to start a conversation. If so, don't worry—you're not alone.

Many people struggle with confidence when it comes to socializing. But the good news is that there are things you can do to build your confidence and make it easier for you to meet new people and make friends. In this chapter, we'll explore some strategies for boosting your confidence so that you can feel more comfortable interacting with others.

What Is Confidence, and Why It's Important for Making Friends?

The ability to create friends is facilitated by self-assurance and high self-esteem. When you're sure of yourself, you radiate positivity and are more willing to initiate contact with people. Even though it may appear that some people are just born with an abundance of self-assurance and radiate confidence, the truth is that anyone can learn to become more comfortable in their own skin and socialize successfully.

What Is Self-Confidence?

Self-confidence can be more situation-specific or relate to a broad belief in your capacity to manage your life (Morin, 2018).

For instance, you could have strong self-confidence in one area of knowledge but low confidence in another.

Self-confidence is the conviction that one can effectively complete the requirements of a given task. It can be challenging to build confidence at times, either because of personal events that have made you doubt yourself or because you have low self-esteem.

How Come Confidence Is Key?

Developing your confidence is a skill that will serve you well, no matter your field of endeavor. Still, it will be especially useful when you feel down. Being confident is essential to attracting and establishing meaningful connections.

It is a necessary skill to interact well with others; it helps you connect with others more quickly and develop lasting relationships.

Principles for Being Confident

Changing your mindset is essential to understand how to boost your self-assurance. Your internal state, or "mood," can be considered a snapshot of your mental condition at any moment. Your current self-esteem impacts how you're feeling, affecting your mood. You can alter your internal state at any time, regardless of what is happening around you, as long as you understand how to do it.

Here are the key ideas for increasing confidence and how to put them into practice:

Body Language

Studying how the body works might help with self-assurance by teaching you to project confidence through your body language. Consider a person you know who you see as being very confident. When you first encountered them, you undoubtedly noticed that they exuded an air of self-assurance even before they began speaking. By the way, they held themselves and walked, you could tell they were confident. They looked you in the eye, shook your hand firmly, and stood tall.

Take a moment to quickly inventory your physique. How do you hold yourself?

Describe your breathing. Everybody experiences bad moods occasionally, which might result in slouching, shallow breathing, or drooping your head. You can change your feelings about yourself by exerting control over how your body behaves and how you carry yourself.

Positivity

Positive thinking has many different manifestations. Change your concentration first because "where focus goes, energy flows." Consider all the potential positive outcomes rather than getting caught up in the negative ones. Consider how fantastic your presentation will be and how happy your coworkers will be to hear it. Your reality is created by your thoughts, including the ones you give the most attention to. Switch out negative terms for positive ones to begin noticing the good aspects of things. You may alter your state by shifting your internal and external emphasis, and you may alter your condition to alter your life.

Control Your Emotions

Humans have a remarkable and exceptional ability to feel various emotions. But only allow your feelings to rule your perception of reality after identifying the source of those feelings.

Your feelings will eventually take control of you, but your feelings, especially your confidence level, are under your control. People don't naturally possess confidence; you have to cultivate it. Gaining confidence gives you the conviction that you can complete the task at hand. Like any other emotion, confidence may be felt. It's a feeling; you can learn to tap into it once you've cultivated it.

A Mindset of Growth

What do you believe having confidence means? You may believe that past achievements are the only way to convey confidence, so you can only believe in yourself after you've achieved significant accomplishments.

This type of thinking severely restricts your growth. Your inner conviction in who you are gives you confidence, not your external accomplishments. Having confidence means not giving up when things get challenging. Your beliefs will gradually take shape as you begin making concrete efforts toward your objective of having confidence. It's time to embrace a growth mentality and realize that self-assurance is a skill that can be achieved.

How to Build Self-Confidence

You may boost your confidence in several ways. These activities might be helpful whether you struggle with confidence in general or in a particular area.

Put an End to Comparing Yourself to Others

Do you judge your appearance based on the Instagram users you follow? Or perhaps you make a salary comparison with your colleague. According to the "social comparison hypothesis," comparing things is normal. However, it's unlikely to help you gain more confidence. There's a chance it'll have the opposite impact.

A study published in 2018 in the journal *Personality and Individual Differences* identified a correlation between envy and low self-esteem (Vrabel et al., 2018). Specifically, studies found that envy occurs when people compare themselves with others. Additionally, people feel worse about themselves the more jealousy they have.

How do you increase your confidence when you become aware that you are making comparisons? Remember first that comparison serves no useful purpose. Everyone is just trying to do what they need to.

Remembering your strengths and accomplishments is beneficial if you're envious of someone else's life. Keep a gratitude notebook to help you remember your life's blessings. This can help redirect your attention to your own life rather than those of others.

Be Around Positive People

Consider how you feel around your current friend group. Do they uplift you or bring you down? Do they always judge you or accept you as you are?

Perhaps more than you know, the company you keep impacts your self-perception and your thoughts and attitudes about yourself. So be aware of how other people affect your mood. It could be time to part ways if you feel self-conscious after spending time with a particular person.

As an alternative, surround yourself with individuals who care about you and want what's best for you. Find people who can boost your confidence and who are optimistic. Confidence in oneself and a positive outlook on life go together (Rafiei et al., 2018).

Look After Your Body

This is based on the notion that abusing your body makes it difficult to think positively about yourself. When you take care of yourself, you'll automatically feel more confident because you'll know that you're taking good care of your mind, body, and soul.

The following self-care activities have been linked to increased confidence levels (*Self-Care Tips for the Body & Soul*, n.d.):

- **Diet**: Eating well has several advantages, including improved confidence and self-esteem. You feel better about yourself when you nourish your body with nutritious meals. You also feel stronger, more energized, and healthier.
- **Exercise**: Research repeatedly demonstrates that engaging in physical activity increases confidence.
- **Meditation**: More than merely a method of stress relief, meditation has several benefits for enhancing self-confidence. One benefit is that it aids in self-awareness and acceptance. Additionally, meditation encourages you to stop doubting yourself and disengage from mind clutter that undermines your confidence.
- **Sleep**: Sound sleep has been associated with positive personality qualities, including optimism and self-worth (Lemola et al., 2012).

Self-care is essential to self-confidence. Ensure that you provide yourself with the resources necessary to have a positive self-image and confidence in your talents.

Be Compassionate to Yourself

Connecting with yourself and others is encouraged by developing emotional flexibility and learning to manage difficult emotions.

Therefore, the next time you find yourself in a difficult circumstance, remember that it is normal to make mistakes and occasionally fall short of your goals. Make every effort to handle these situations with kindness toward yourself.

Use Constructive Self-Talk

By persuading your subconscious that something is "too hard" for you to manage or that you "shouldn't even attempt," negative self-talk may restrict your talents and undermine your self-confidence.

Contrarily, positive self-talk can promote self-compassion, assist in overcoming self-doubt, and encourage you to approach new people.

Here are some strategies for combating negative internal dialogue and replacing it with constructive, confidence-boosting thoughts:

- *"I can't do it,"* or *"It's impossible,"* transforms into *"Actually, I can do it,"* or *"All I should do is try."*
- *"I can't accomplish anything properly,"* it is transformed into *"I'll do things differently from now on,"* or *"But at least I learned something in the process."*
- *"I dread public speaking. It's awful!"* becomes, *"I try to avoid public speaking* because *All of us have strengths and limitations."*

Practice What You're Good At

According to one study, life satisfaction levels are marginally correlated with confidence in your ability to capitalize on your qualities (Tsai et al., 2014). Finding out just what strengths you have is the first step.

Make a list of your strengths and make a conscious effort to keep practicing and perfecting them. You'll become more confident once you see how talented you are.

The Art of Saying "No"

While doing what you're excellent at might enhance your self-assurance, it's equally crucial to be aware of circumstances that could make you lose confidence. You may have noticed that engaging in a particular pastime consistently leaves you feeling down on yourself rather than up.

It's okay to say no to things that tend to make you feel unhappy. Yes, you should be open to things that challenge you in order to grow. However, there is nothing wrong with setting boundaries.

Setting limits in social and emotional areas makes you feel psychologically safer. You may feel more in charge of things. Feeling in charge of your life is a key component of self-confidence (*What Is Self-Confidence?* 2022). And the act of setting boundaries helps create this sense of being in control.

Set Attainable Objectives

When pursuing your objectives, it's common to experience several failures before figuring out what works. This may cause you to doubt your ability to achieve them in the end. Realistic goal-setting is the key.

Confidence levels have been shown to suffer when ambitious goals are set and not met (Höpfner & Keith, 2021). On the other hand, attainable goals are practical. And as you accomplish your goals, you'll feel more confident in your skills and talents.

Write out your objectives so that you can create more achievable goals. Then, ask yourself what your chances are of achieving it (be sincere!). The objective could be slightly overly ambitious if the response is slim to none. Reduce it to a level that is more attainable and reasonable.

A review of how we can build our confidence over time:

- Start believing in yourself.
- Identify your strengths and weaknesses.
- Practice positive self-talk, and don't be too hard on yourself.
- Celebrate your accomplishments, both big and small.
- Visualize yourself achieving your goal.
- Practice self-compassion when things don't go as planned.

How to Act Confident Even if You Don't Feel It at First

You know those times when you're doing something significant, perhaps even quite thrilling, but secretly you're kind of terrified? Most of us would do whatever we could to project confidence in those situations, even if we didn't feel it. Because the circumstances that scare us frequently include things that are really significant to us.

Being confident and developing confidence are key components of seeming confident. Here are some strategies for seeming confident even when you're not:

- Fake it until you make it.
- Stand up tall and straight.
- Make eye contact with people when you speak to them.
- Smile even if you don't feel like it.
- Pretend you know what you're doing, even if you don't.
- Take deep breaths and relax your body.
- Repeat positive affirmations to yourself.

Ways to Stay Confident When Things Get Tough

Everybody experiences difficult days or upsetting times. It's also important to remember that being confident doesn't mean you always know what you're doing. Building confidence is less about having all the answers and more about knowing that you can deal with whatever comes your way and grow from the experience.

Remember the following when faced with a tough situation:

- Don't compare yourself to others, as this will only lead to feeling inferior.
- Focus on being the best version of yourself.
- Be yourself—don't try to be someone you're not—accept yourself for who you are.

Key elements of this chapter:

- Confidence is believing in yourself and your abilities.
- When you feel confident, it will show in your body language and how you speak.

- Being confident doesn't mean you're always right—admitting when you're wrong is okay.
- Confidence is something that can be learned and improved over time.
- With practice, you'll be able to build lasting relationships with the people around you.

Now that you know that confidence is critical and how to cultivate yours, we need to discuss the topic of charisma.

CHAPTER 5:

BECOMING MORE CHARISMATIC

Charisma... It's that certain *je ne sais quoi* that some people have, and others don't. But what is charisma, really? Is it something that can be learned? The answer to both questions is a resounding "yes!" Charisma is the ability to charm, inspire, and motivate others. It's a quality that can be helpful in both your personal and professional life.

Charisma Demystified

Have you ever encountered a person with a particular "presence" that sets them apart? Someone who immediately made you feel special, accepted, and significant? The sort of person who makes you question whether you would rather be in their presence or take their place in the world. Most of the time, this "it" factor or "presence" is high charisma.

But for those who don't have charisma, there are ways to develop it. In this section, we'll examine the connection between the three factors—presence, power, and warmth—that contribute to charisma and, ultimately, how to develop it.

The term "charisma" refers to a unique attribute in some personalities typically characterized by great appeal, a "magnetic" element to one's personality or looks, and natural and highly developed personal communicability and persuasiveness. In other words, charisma is frequently used to describe the remarkable capacity to influence or persuade others (*Charisma*, 2020).

Someone with a charming personality possesses both leadership and social abilities. They captivate and influence people with their warmth and skill. They use self-awareness, open body language, listen intently, and respect everyone, all behavioral learning skills.

It doesn't matter whether you are (or aren't) conventionally beautiful, outgoing, or introverted or if you have numerous jokes up your sleeve. You can learn how to be charismatic!

People are more likely to be persuaded by someone with a charismatic personality because they perceive them as reliable, amiable, and completely present. Playing to their talents in any social setting is how charismatic individuals show that they are kind and competent.

A summary of demystified charisma:

- Charisma is not a magical quality that some people are born with and others are not.
- Anyone can learn to be more charismatic.
- To be more charismatic, you need to work on all three elements simultaneously.
- Practice makes perfect. The more you practice, the better you'll become at being charismatic.

Key Elements of Being Charismatic: Presence, Power, and Warmth

The three primary components of charismatic behavior are presence, power, and warmth.

These components rely on our deliberately chosen behaviors and unconsciously controlled variables. This section will examine how these various signals can be impacted. We must adopt mental states that produce the body language, words, and behaviors that collectively convey these essential components of charisma if we want to be more charismatic.

The subject we'll discuss in this section is:

- Presence is about making a good first impression and being confident in yourself.
- Power is about projecting authority and being in control.
- Warmth is about being friendly and likable.

Presence

Do you frequently notice yourself nodding off while listening to someone speak? Perhaps you notice that when you're speaking, your eyes wander? The absence of presence is the cause of these behaviors. It's harder to seem to be listening or paying attention than you may believe because others can notice these expressions in milliseconds (Cabane, 2013).

People feel dismissed, irritated, inferior, and even angry when they observe this lack of presence (Cabane, 2013). Additionally, this absence of a physical presence might be seen as dishonest, which has even worse emotional repercussions. It is extremely difficult to foster trust and cultivate authentic relationships and loyalty if you are perceived as being untrue to yourself and others.

Why Are We So Absent?

Our brains are wired neurologically to pay attention to unknown stimuli (Cabane, 2013). Thanks to this wiring, humans could maintain their sense of caution and survive throughout evolution. However, charisma is not an adaptive trait in the evolutionary sense.

Second, distractions are a significant part of our culture. We are glued to our phones and continuously exposed to stimulants. This exacerbates our inclinations and results in a condition of partial attention that seems unavoidable (Cabane, 2013). Learning to become an active listener is our best solution!

Establishing Presence

A study of 2,250 people indicated that "mind-wandering" takes up approximately 50% of a person's time (Gilbert, 2009). This proportion comprises all regular communications and activities, including typical conversation and meditation. But like many other characteristics, presence is a talent that can be learned. Practice sharpening your concentration as a handy mindfulness exercise to enhance your present (Cabane, 2013).

How to be more present:

- **Put sound first**. Examine your surroundings while listening. You may be more alert and present if you take in every sound you hear.
- **Concentrate on breathing**. You may improve your awareness of your body's position by concentrating on the "in" and "out" of breathing. Additionally, it aids in drowning out any unnecessary noises that distract you from what must be focused on.

- **Pay attention to your lower body**. Your mind is compelled to go through your complete body if you concentrate on a specific part of your lower body, like your toes. You'll become more conscious of your bodily expressions and motions.

Next time you're having a discussion, check in with yourself every so often to observe where your thoughts are wandering. The capacity to be present makes you more memorable during new encounters. It fosters an emotional connection, which contributes to your sense of charisma.

Practice is all it takes to develop the habit of putting everything else aside to talk and listen to others. For those two, three, or ten minutes, you only think about those things as you narrow down your attention to them.

People you are with will feel as though they have your undivided attention and that, at that one time, they are everything to you. This is the key to being charismatic in front of other people. Now that you understand what presence may be and how to put yourself out there, let's talk about power and warmth.

Power

Another element of charisma is perceived power; being powerful is to be seen as having a significant impact on the world around us, whether by our control over it, our influence over it, our wealth, our physical prowess, or our high social position. It is crucial to always be aware of your look and body language since these are two areas where others can usually tell how powerful you are.

Establishing Power

Speak at a slower, lower tone since this is a straightforward technique to project a forceful presence. A recent study looked at how speech and voice tones affect how dominant and prestigious we perceive someone to be (Kalkhoff et al., 2017). College students on research panels were shown edited transcripts of interviews, and they evaluated the presenters' and the guests' degrees of prestige and dominance. The findings demonstrated that undertone-rich sounds were perceived as more powerful and alluring. People who spoke more slowly and with deeper resonances were automatically given leadership roles.

- **Speak softly and slowly.** People who speak more slowly and quietly may have more influence and charm in social situations. When people interact with high-status individuals, they attempt to mimic their tones (Morgan, 2014). We seek to match individuals who are strong or in positions of authority and those on the same "level" as ourselves. As a result, when given the option to choose a leader, people frequently select someone with the appropriate voice. You will undoubtedly develop some charm and a strong presence if you learn to generate this voice of a leader.

Warmth

The final component of charisma is warmth. One's level of warmth indicates how willing they are to assist others in need.

Being seen as kind, compassionate, selfless, and eager to take constructive action may be defined as having warmth toward others (Cabane, 2013). It may also be seen through body language; however, unlike power, warmth is evaluated more immediately and primarily through conduct and body language.

Creating a Warmer Persona

It is not unexpected that meeting people in person fosters warmth and empathy, given that it is sociable. Researchers have shown that college students now exhibit far less empathy than they did 40 years ago, with the sharpest loss occurring around 2000 (Konrath et al., 2011). They explained this 40% drop in empathy by the fall in face-to-face interaction brought on by the spread of social media.

The facial expressions of other people cause our brains to become more empathic. On the other hand, our empathy levels fall when we lose part of these encounters. To develop the kind of empathetic, affable demeanor essential to charm, taking time away from your screen and engaging in real-world interactions with other people is essential.

Charismatic Body Language

The ability to communicate effectively is only possible if you have been schooled in the science of body language. Here are some strategies to help you start improving your body language readings and communication abilities (Thorp, 2016):

- **Create a connection.** Building and sustaining connections is one very crucial thing to keep in mind. The simplest way to describe connection is to think of it as your way of connecting with or relating to people, particularly when it comes to sociable relationships.
- **Establish eye contact.** When speaking to someone, remember to look them in the eyes. It's also crucial to keep eye contact when listening. They will feel heard and acknowledged as a result of this.
- **Decrease the distance.** To communicate with the other person, remove all barriers. When engaging with an individual face-to-face, the office might require you to turn around to the other side of the desk. Or, instead of shouting across the room, just step into the same room where the person is. This will contribute to fostering a feeling of respect and closeness.
- **Maintain good posture.** Maintain a straight posture while you speak and listen. Avoid crossing your arms since doing so might be interpreted as angry or closed-off. Even our bodies' inclination toward the person must be taken into consideration. Leaning backward might convey disinterest, whereas leaning forward displays interest in their communication.
- **Observe yourself.** Be mindful of your facial expressions while listening and communicating. You may practice this by talking to yourself in the mirror as though you were speaking to a friend. Practice exchanging ideas in relational, social, and professional contexts. Pay attention to how your expression changes when you communicate.
- **Be intentional.** Another critical topic is the motivation behind anything you are expressing. When your head and heart are connected, it's easy to modify your body language.

Think about the message you want to convey and the effect you want it to have on the other person.

- **Be adaptable.** Feel free to try a new approach to communicating verbally or through body language if your intended message or point needs to be understood. You can change your direction any time if you're prepared to adapt to what is and isn't working. If you feel that your tone is too high-pitched, simply adjust it to a lower pitch.

Remember that every person has a unique method of interpreting communication. We frequently speak with people in the manner we prefer to be addressed. In other words, we think everyone should act or react as we would. That is not always the case. Every person communicates and is communicated with differently. Keeping this in mind can help you master the subtle but crucial art of communication and, more significantly, the skill of communicating with your body.

Here is a quick guide to the essential things to remember to appear charismatic in conversation:

- Mirror the other person's body language.
- Lean in when the other person is talking.
- Use open body language (spread your arms, uncross your legs).
- Make eye contact.
- Smile!

Do your best to speak from the heart and be as adaptable as possible. Keep in mind that our intentions heavily influence our non-verbal communication. Since nonverbal communication is spontaneous and, for the most part, unconscious, we aren't consciously aware of our posture or our expressions when we are listening to others, whether intentionally or not. Our emotional state also directly affects how others see us; our body language can hint at or express it openly, so we should choose to convey a positive state of mind.

On Being More Charismatic

To be viewed as charismatic by others, it is essential to have a friendly demeanor, frequently use the person's name while speaking to them, and smile and make eye contact. Additionally, you'll become likable if you connect with them by paying close attention to what they say, embracing their quirks and imperfections, and looking for areas of similarity.

It's crucial to remain authentic as you develop charm, even if that means avoiding stressful public events in favor of more personal settings where you can converse clearly. Without genuine curiosity and concern for other people, charisma would never fully develop.

Here are a few more things to consider as you discover your charismatic side:

- Control your anxiety.
- Be approachable.
- Carry yourself with a lighthearted attitude.
- Do not forget names.
- Ask more questions.
- Be interested in other people and what they have to say.
- Don't be judgmental or critical of others.
- Listen more than you talk.
- Show enthusiasm when you're talking about something you're passionate about.

The most efficient framework for maximizing your charm potential combines the three behaviors of presence, power, and warmth. Your affability (how easily you can connect with others emotionally) and your ability to exert influence are crucial components of charisma (your ability to motivate others). It isn't about being so kind that you give in to any and all requests or even tolerate rudeness from other people, and it's not about being submissive when you should be assertive. Being charismatic means continually expressing who you are, whether loudly or subtly. Sometimes it's as simple as just being there.

CHAPTER 6:

IMPROVE YOUR SOCIAL SKILLS

Making friends can be hard, but it's worth it because friends make life more gratifying and fun! If you're having trouble making friends, it might be because your social skills could use some work. Don't worry, though—you can do plenty of things to improve your social skills!

What Are Social Skills?

Children and adults might struggle with social skills, resulting in anxiety and severe phobias. Adults who struggle with social skills may avoid social situations and have trouble forming long-lasting connections.

Our ability to connect, communicate, and form relationships depends on our social skills. They may also be referred to as "interpersonal" or "people skills."

Every day, people interact with one another in several ways, including verbally, nonverbally, in writing, and visually.

While nonverbal communication is done through body language, facial expressions, and eye contact, verbal abilities focus only on spoken words. You use your social skills every time you communicate with another person. Strong social skills will give you the edge to communicate effectively with anyone and help you make life-long connections with others.

Emotional Intelligence Is the Social Cornerstone

Emotional intelligence (EI) is the capacity to notice your feelings, identify feelings in others, and then use those feelings to guide your behavior. Cultivating your emotional intelligence can help you better understand and manage social interactions (Ravenscraft, 2020).

There are several theories on how to develop emotional intelligence. However, we will focus on the five key skills of Daniel Goleman's emotional intelligence framework (Ravenscraft, 2020).

The five key social skills that you need to master are:

- **Self-Awareness:** Being able to name your feelings and understand how they function. Do noisy surroundings make you nervous? Do you get mad when someone interrupts you? You are engaging in self-awareness if you are aware of these aspects of yourself. This is easier said than done, but the first step is becoming conscious of your thoughts and feelings.
- **Self-Regulation:** Going a step further, this concept has to do with your capacity to recognize and control your emotions. Understanding how to cool down is helpful if you are frustrated; self-regulation can help you deal with feelings you might experience.
- **Motivation:** External reasons such as money, status, or suffering can be potent motivators. Internal motivation, however, plays a significant role in Goleman's concept. This implies that you learn how to keep yourself motivated and start or keep working on projects because you want to, not because someone else wants you to. You take action because you want to, not because you have to.
- **Empathy:** It's just as crucial to understand how other people feel as it is to know how you feel. This could mean learning to acknowledge how individuals express themselves. For example, can you distinguish between someone who is comfortable and someone who is nervous? It also means knowing how people might react to the situations they find themselves in.
- **Socialization:** This concept is about how well you can manage relationships and get along with others. It doesn't mean controlling other people, but knowing how to achieve your objectives alongside others. That could mean telling your coworkers about your ideas, leading a group, or solving a problem in a relationship.

There isn't always a "right" approach to handling every social setting because they are unique. But when you look at most social situations through the lens of these key skills, they become much easier to handle.

What should you take from this?

- Social skills are the ability to interact with others respectfully, politely, and considerately.
- Social skills involve being able to understand and respond to the emotions of others.
- Social skills include communicating effectively with others, both verbally and non-verbally.
- People who have good social skills are typically able to make friends easily and maintain healthy relationships.
- People who lack social skills often find it challenging to connect with others and can sometimes be seen as socially awkward or shy.

Now, how do you know if your social skills need a bit of an upgrade? Anyone seeking to establish personal and professional connections should work on their social skills (yes, that includes you too).

Do Your Social Skills Need Improvement?

In contrast to more theoretical fields like math and physics, social skills are best acquired through hands-on experience. Through play, children can experience social interaction and develop skills in dispute resolution, friend-making, and group dynamics. However, only some have the same method for grasping concepts. They can also take a lifetime to perfect.

Learning social skills might be challenging if you didn't grow up with exposure to typical group dynamics, if you suffer from a mental disease like depression or anxiety, or if you just didn't have many positive role models. Through social interaction, young individuals often learn how to control their emotions, identify others' emotions, and effectively control them. Don't worry if you didn't learn these abilities as a child. Know that you are not alone.

If you're unsure whether or not your social skills could use some work, here are a few signs that might indicate that you need to work on your social skills:

- You find it hard to relate to others and often feel like an outsider.
- You're unsure how to continue a conversation or end one gracefully.
- While other people talk to you, you keep scrolling through your phone.
- You tend to say the wrong thing or put your foot in your mouth a lot.
- You have trouble reading other people's emotions or body language.
- You always wear headphones (in an attempt to avoid conversation).
- You never meet up with anyone in person.
- You try to make people laugh when it's not the right time.
- You're not good at asking questions or showing interest in other people.

Now that we've established that we "all" need to work on our social skills, what is the next step in improving them?

How to Improve Social Skills

Learning how to better interact with others is a skill that will serve you well in all aspects of your life. Social skills are crucial since they may improve the effectiveness and efficiency of your communication. You can develop, maintain, and create more meaningful connections with colleagues, friends, and others.

What should you take from this section?

- Learn how to have fluid and interesting conversations with anyone, anywhere.
- Learn to read people's social cues and respond appropriately.
- Start developing your empathy muscles, which will make you a better listener.
- Avoid feeling awkward in any social situation.

- Learn how to start and maintain conversations.
- Understand nonverbal communication.

What is the quickest route to improving your social skills? Build your mental muscle memory! Learn to use your emotions to your advantage and select words (both those you used to connect with others and those that tell you) that will assist you in making new connections.

Your First Impression

The most crucial thing to remember is that how you make people feel in those initial few seconds after meeting them is far more memorable than how you appear.

Consider this: Do you not have a gut reaction to new acquaintances, positive or negative? For me, it's a result of both their mood and outward appearance.

Do they perceive your actions as trustworthy and confident enough to believe in you? Are you showing that you're interested in making eye contact and using your body language? Do you exhibit sensitivity to others and a lack of self-interest?

As the saying goes, first impressions are everything. Whether you like it or not, your social skills will have a significant impact on the impression you make.

If You're Shy, Start Early

If you're shy, you should aim to introduce yourself to someone in the room as soon as you walk in. This will prevent you from being anxious since you have already broken the shy person's bubble.

Many of us worry about our nervousness, what other people think of us, and our fear of coming across as ignorant. In actuality, a lot of them have similar thoughts about themselves. So don't be scared to make the first move!

The Significance of Small Talk

I learned something new from this one. Do you fit the stereotype of the person who prefers to cut to the chase and avoid "wasting time" with useless chit-chat? Knowing that small talk makes it possible for people to view you as a whole person instead of a lifeless and rigid person. Putting yourself out there and making connections are two important differentiators to help you make new friends.

Taking Small Steps

To enhance your social abilities, practice conversing with the people you see regularly. A checkout clerk could ask you how your day is going while shopping, and you might respond with a question rather than a one-word response. The same is true for finding methods to extend talks with acquaintances or honing your conversational skills with distant relatives with whom you don't speak frequently.

Raise Open-Ended Questions

Open-ended inquiries may be a powerful tool for getting people to talk. It may be helpful since it will give you understanding and insight into your loved ones, coworkers, new acquaintances, and friends. Interacting with someone with an open-ended inquiry may be beneficial for your relationship-building efforts since it can make them feel as though their views and emotions are genuine.

People frequently like open-ended questions since they demonstrate your interest in their opinions.

Try the following free-form questions:

- What are your thoughts on...?
- Can you elaborate on...?
- Why do you think that?

Develop Your Listening Skills

An excellent method to keep a discussion going is to ask open-ended questions but use caution. When you interrogate someone excessively, you risk appearing robotic or uninterested. You don't want someone to believe you aren't paying attention to them.

How do you listen, though? It takes more than simply passively taking in information to listen effectively. You should instead demonstrate that you are paying attention to the other person. This is communicated through affirmative speech, positive body language, and appropriate amounts of quiet.

Start by confirming what the other individual is expressing. Suppose someone describes their upbringing in a foreign nation, for instance. In that case, you can respond, "That does give you a distinct perspective on..."

This positive comment shows that you are listening and considering what you hear.

The use of body language follows. The following nonverbal cues indicate that you are paying attention:

- Turning to face each other (don't turn away or stare into space).
- Nodding your head.
- Direct eye contact.

Lastly, try to limit your speaking. Be calm, pay attention, and listen to the other person's words.

Don't Try to Be Funny

Making friends by being hilarious is a terrific idea. However, not everyone can laugh. At least, not everybody has a constant sense of humor. Everyone doesn't share that personality. Having meaningful conversations and creating genuine relationships is possible without being funny. Serious individuals are also needed and have a place in the world.

Avoid attempting to impose comedy in any way. When you're attempting to be hilarious, people can tell. Just be who you are. You'll discover that just by chatting, you'll inevitably make someone chuckle.

Examine the Social Skills of Others

Observing others is another way to improve your social abilities. To start a conversation, pay attention to nonverbal cues, body language (such as smiling and nodding), and the terminology they use. Think about what makes their social skills engaging and successful. These findings might be a reference point for improving your communication skills further.

Give Compliments That Are True and Sincere

A fantastic method of showing kindness and respect for people is complimenting them when they do a good deed. Compliments might also serve as the start or continuation of a dialogue. Be honest because flattery that isn't earned might backfire.

Research Resources for Social Skills

You may enhance social skills through online and offline courses, publications, podcasts, and tools. Look up information on a particular subject, such as body language, networking, or active listening. Be sure to put your newfound knowledge into practice.

Stay Updated on Happenings

Keeping up with current events, trends, and news items may provide you with conversation starters. Think about signing up for newsletters unique to your sector or local news to have content at your fingertips.

Develop Your Closing Skills

Knowing how to start a conversation with grace and comfort is a crucial component of having excellent social skills. You don't want to "get stuck" in that conversation after you've started it, as in spending 40 minutes conversing with the same individual at the cocktail party. You should also be able to wrap things up gracefully.

Saying, "It was a pleasure meeting you," is all you need to say after the conversation has run its course or you've reached your attention limits. Thank them for the conversation, then make your exit. Your attitude is crucial while delivering that little two-liner. You can grin, but you also need to start backing off.

Additional Tips

- Attend social events.
- Talk to people you don't know.
- Join a club or group that meets your interests.
- Volunteer for a project or organization.
- Take a class on social skills or communication.
- Practice your conversation starters and icebreakers.
- Get feedback from others on how you can improve your social skills.

You'll develop greater confidence as your social encounters go better. Additionally, socializing will become more straightforward (and enjoyable!) as your confidence grows. But if you don't put yourself out there and try, you can't improve your skills.

Developing your social skills will set you on the right path. You must accept that developing these skills will take time. Before you can confidently use them in social situations, you will need to put in the time to learn them and practice them consistently.

CHAPTER 7:

WHERE TO FIND NEW FRIENDS

Finding new friends can be daunting. It can be challenging to know where to start or how to go about meeting new people. However, there are several ways to meet new friends, and it is essential to be creative and open-minded.

Knowing where to search is part of the difficulty of meeting new friends. People tend to write off the possibility of making friends because they believe there are none to be found. But finding friends is not the issue; making an effort to do so is.

Here are some places where you might meet potential connections:

Attend Local Music Concerts, Culinary Classes, or Artistic Festivals

One of the finest methods to make new acquaintances is to go to festivals. Festivals are highly social events emphasizing enjoyment and frequently featuring team sports, contests, and performances. You can browse an events calendar on the website of your town or city's newspaper.

Join a Sports Team or the Gym

It is predictable to propose going to the gym to meet people. However, it is something that individuals frequently do. Get active by signing up for a gym membership or a league for grownups. You can also check whether a baseball, soccer, kickball, bowling, or tennis team exists and join up.

Do a Road Race in Your Area

Road races are enjoyable, friendly social gatherings, as any runner will attest to. Races and running groups provide enjoyable opportunities to make new friends, experience your area from a different angle, and work up a sweat.

Participating in the running community has advantages for experienced and inexperienced runners (don't worry, it's not an elite group!).

You may connect with another athlete in your region through an app such as Nike Run Club, compete against them, or simply cheer them on.

Sign Up for a Club

Joining a local club is a fantastic way to make new friends.

Additionally, discussing the subjects you are enthusiastic about can help you get to know one another much better. If you join a club, you will, at the very least, have several individuals with whom you can socialize regularly, even if you do not wind up meeting the person who will become your closest friend in that club.

Sign Up for a Wine Club

You won't have any trouble striking up conversations and making friends at a wine club if you appreciate fine wine and stimulating conversation.

There are wine clubs in several places that visit the neighborhood wineries and restaurants (where applicable). Along the way, meet friends and learn more about wine!

Be Part of a Book Club

In addition to being one of the finest venues for making new friends, book clubs are also an excellent method for reading for mental and emotional well-being.

Join a book club where you can meet new people and relax each month with a different book. Start searching for nearby book clubs at your neighborhood bookshop or public library. You might even create your book club if there is yet to be one already established in your community.

Use Social Media

Social media aims to connect individuals. A person's social media profiles are a gold mine for reconnecting with people they may not have seen since high school or elsewhere. Even though you are already "friends" with someone online, if you notice anything they post that piques your curiosity, get in touch with them.

Social media may be used to plan gatherings as well. If you want to arrange a poker night, post something on social media to see if anyone is interested.

Join Facebook Groups

Joining an online community on Facebook is among the finest methods to find friends online. To refine your search, type what you're looking for in the site's top search box, then click "groups."

To view results for your city, try to include your city's name in the search.

Apps for Friends

To meet new individuals, some people use apps for platonic companionship. This could make interacting with others less daunting. Examples in use today are Nextdoor and Bumble BFF. Browse the web or app store for additional possibilities.

Join Meetup.com

Joining MeetUp.com may be among the finest strategies to make new acquaintances. You may input your city and interests on this internet forum to browse an infinite number of "meetups" nearby.

Speak to Your Neighbors

A surprising number of individuals are blissfully unaware that they may be becoming friends with someone who lives directly next door to them or just across the street from them. They wave politely and then shut their door without attempting to initiate a conversation. However, you could find some very fantastic friendships just next door. When you two are next together, make some effort beyond merely waving.

Take Your Pet to the Park

An immediate conversation starter is a mutual love of animals. If you and your dog are fans of the great outdoors, going to a dog park together is likely to be one of the most enjoyable ways for you to make new friends.

Is there none nearby? If making friends in a new location is on your to-do list, take your dog for a walk in a bustling area like downtown to increase your chances of meeting new people.

Enjoy a Day Outdoors

Lay on a beach towel with a good book and take in some rays, or play volleyball with a group of possible friends. Spending time alone at a beach or lake might be an excellent pastime. Still, it also provides many opportunities to meet new people and make new acquaintances.

Think about enrolling in a water-based class, such as paddleboarding or snorkeling, and using these pursuits to make friends.

Get To Know Your Coworkers

Your coworkers are people you spend a lot of time with.

Furthermore, even though you are in a business situation, you probably already know a lot about one another.

When appropriate, invite a coworker out for a fun activity that has nothing to do with business, even if you don't physically work together. Suggest going to a baseball game together, for instance, or going to dinner after work. Consider doing something you both enjoy together, like yoga or cooking.

Attend a Networking or Meet-up Event

Meet-ups and other networking opportunities are excellent opportunities to meet fresh faces, whether you work remotely or travel to a workplace every day. These gatherings are not only crowded with professionals eager to network, but they are also fantastic settings for meeting others who have similar interests.

Make Conversation With Other Parents

You probably spend a lot of time at parks, on movie lines, and eating far too much pizza if you look after young children. Parents may be just as snobbish as children, so don't let them scare you if you see them chit-chatting on the playground or in the park. Use your children as a discussion starter while establishing acquaintances as adults since you share a frame of reference with them. Ask for thoughts on the homework assignment, the school's uniform rules (or lack thereof), and any other child-related matter that comes to mind. The worst that may happen is that you'll only speak to someone once before moving on. In a perfect world, you would find each other, enjoy each other's company, and eventually develop a friendship.

Involve Yourself in Your Religious Community

Visiting a church, mosque, or synagogue, even if it's been years, is a terrific opportunity to reconnect with individuals who share your beliefs.

Additionally, there are frequently several options for participation. If you're seeking a place to mingle and make new acquaintances, look no further than your local house of worship.

Volunteer

One excellent strategy to increase your sense of thankfulness is volunteering your time and effort. If you put in the time to volunteer, you'll eventually meet others who share your ideals and who will make great friends.

Finding individuals who share your enthusiasm for giving back is simple when you have that desire. If you volunteer for an organization once a month, you'll get the rewards and help the organization.

Volunteering for a good cause is one of the best ways to connect with like-minded people.

Think about some of these deserving causes, for example:

- Advocacy for human rights.
- Kids and young people.
- Animal protection.
- Culture and the arts.
- Literacy and learning.

- Crisis assistance or emergency help.

You can locate a volunteer opportunity that fits you by visiting one of the many volunteer resource centers in your community.

Make Local Purchases

Members of the local business community are always looking to make new friends and provide better service to their neighbors.

You may establish connections with the hard-working business owners in your area by spending time in the neighborhood stores and eateries.

By supporting these establishments, you may also get to know other locals who also "buy local" and maybe form a shopping group.

Visit a Local Farmer's Market

Monthly farmer's markets in several communities offer top-notch local goods and food. Similar to the benefits of shopping locally, visiting a farmer's market is a great opportunity to meet friendly neighbors who share your passion for supporting your local economy.

Due to the variety of individuals that attend, farmer's markets are among the finest places to make new acquaintances if you value a healthy lifestyle.

Visit a Nearby Brewery

The popularity of craft beer has skyrocketed in the past few years, and now there is a brewery in seemingly every city. These breweries serve amazing beer and frequently provide tours and workshops, making them fantastic places to socialize and have fun.

It's typical for adults to have trouble finding new acquaintances. However, making an effort to expand your social network could benefit your mental and emotional well-being. Finding people who share your interests is a fantastic place to start. You can engage in many activities to meet new people. Finding events and clubs in your area is a good place to begin.

There is no right or wrong way to meet new friends! So strike up that conversation on the bus or in your local coffee shop, start a blog or podcast, invite interesting individuals that might make good friends, get to know them, and finally, host that party you've wanted for ages and invite some cool people over to your place! Positivity, authenticity, and a willingness to make new friends are all virtues. You'll quickly feel at home and make genuine friendships with others who share your interests.

CHAPTER 8:

CHOOSING THE RIGHT FRIENDS

It can be challenging to make friends. And it's even harder to find friends who are a good fit for you. But it's important to choose your friends wisely. Only some people you meet will make compatible friends.

What Does It Mean to Be a Good Friend?

In your lifetime, friendships are among your most significant and influential connections. Friends are someone you can confide in and share intimate details with; you play a significant role in each other's life. They make you feel secure and at home because you know that the people you care about adore and cherish you.

The best thing about friendship is that you get to pick your pals, unlike with family. But as anybody who has ever had a bad encounter with someone they believed was a friend will confirm, it isn't always simple to recognize genuine friendship.

You Can Always Rely on Your Friends

Most friendships entail a trustworthy friend who is always there for you, whether with discreet words or overt actions. Because you relocated farther away or lost money, a friend won't abandon you. No matter what stage of life you two are in, best friends are aware that life will provide many challenges, and they will remain with you through them. A true friendship endures these difficulties and remains solid, even when other relationships interfere. A genuine friend sticks by your side during these difficult times.

They Hear You Out

You can be frank and vulnerable with a good friend. This is true because friends help and are trusted by one another.

They Make You Happy Just by Being in Their Presence

A good friend is someone you look forward to hanging out with and who, more significantly, makes you feel confident in social situations where you would not otherwise excel. Genuine friendships are unaffected by this. In the presence of close friends, your self-confidence is at its highest.

They Have a Great Deal of Compassion for You

A good friend is sympathetic to your difficulties or what you are going through and demonstrates their concern by acknowledging your sentiments. Although men and women have different inclinations when sharing feelings, male friends also express their emotions.

They Forgive

Arguments are likely in a long friendship, and good friends are aware of this. They can move on and forgive each other. Genuine friends can recover from practically anything, as most adults eventually discover, especially older individuals or those in their late youth.

Providing What We Can When We Can

Is it possible that the qualities of a good friend have nothing to do with how frequently or how much we see one another? What if a strong friendship was established based on intentionality and giving to each other when we could?

It takes time and effort to master this. It takes patience, kindness, and imagination to be in love; it is a skill that must be developed. Even in the best of circumstances, it is bumpy and rough. The more forgiving we can be toward [our] imperfect humanity, the greater the chance of fulfilling the task of loving (Christian, 2021).

The basis of friendships is the same grace. These connections need us to be present and realize we're all flawed.

Is it necessary to talk to our friends about our relationship requirements and expectations? Yes, of course. The foundation of a strong friendship is open communication and dependability. Our relationships will benefit more the sooner we acknowledge everyone's limitations. This alleviates stress for everyone concerned.

A good friend is someone willing to grow with their friend. We all face unique hurdles while trying to make and maintain friendships. How much we're willing to suffer together ultimately depends on us.

No friendship can last very long when it is stagnant or on autopilot.

Over time, our friendships change in a variety of ways. The process of progress might occasionally seem instinctive, even natural, like leaning toward the wind. Other times, it could be unpleasant, forcing you both to engage in difficult discussions and emotional work. It strengthens, improves, and hardens your connection each time you stretch together.

Even when we try, we cannot duplicate good friendships since they are unique. Every friendship has its own set of rules, restrictions, and moments when it strains and becomes strained. Generally, you can't transfer your friendship-related actions from one to the other.

When we grow, we inevitably break a little bit, and that's okay, too. Even over distance, a good friend serves as both a secure haven and a confidante who pushes us to improve and face our flaws. Everyone needs someone to help them see when they are getting in their way. Here, discernment is needed since, eventually, we must choose what's best for us. But in times of adversity, a close friend may act as a compass.

And occasionally, our friendships serve to distance us from one another. However, as nothing lasts forever, this might signify a strong friendship.

Even though a challenging friendship isn't always undesirable, it's essential to consider the benefits and drawbacks of the friendship. While challenging, it is acceptable to leave a friendship with grace. It doesn't imply that either of you is an awful friend; you are just distant acquaintances who are now only remembered in memories and the occasional "happy birthday" message. When the moment is right, good friends might say goodbye.

The foundation of a good friendship is intention, honesty, and providing others with a secure space where they may be silent for a time and take a break when needed.

What it means to be a good friend:

- Friends should be supportive and positive.
- They should be good listeners and offer constructive advice.
- Friends should make you feel comfortable and accepted for who you are.
- They should be able to have fun and enjoy life.
- Friendships take work: both people need to put in the effort to maintain the relationship.
- Good friends are worth keeping, even if they're not perfect.

So, you know what it takes to be a good friend, but how would you know if someone is a good fit for you?

Are They a Good Fit for You?

The people you choose to spend time with should have specific fundamental characteristics, like the ones listed below.

Make Friends Who Share Your Values

While having a variety of friendships has many advantages, keeping close relationships with those who share your fundamental beliefs is essential. Even if you can tolerate other people's viewpoints and differences, sticking with friends who share the same values can help you avoid making compromises or being negatively influenced by those who do not. Friends that share the same values can help one another stay accountable.

If you want to succeed, you should surround yourself with others who are also pushing themselves to improve. If the only people in your life who supported you were uninspired, how could they urge you to keep trying when you don't prevail? You can become discouraged and forget your goals.

It's essential to have friends who can listen to your concerns and encourage you to keep going, especially if they're in a similar situation. This kind of friend is also fantastic at praising your achievements without showing envy.

Select Friends Who Can Counterbalance Your Weaknesses

Each of us has unique abilities and restrictions (do you already know yours?). Having the appropriate friends allows you to use their knowledge, experience, and expertise in areas where you may be lacking.

Pick a Friend Who Will Stand By You Through Hard Times

When circumstances are good, it's easy for us to become amazing friends. There are many funny and joyful times, and those situations strengthen connections. But who offers you support when circumstances are challenging? You may honestly call those people your friends.

They understand that things rarely turn out the way we expect them to. It makes sense to select a friend who would instead support you in all your endeavors and whom you can grieve with. This is because it is more challenging to stick with anyone at a challenging time.

Select a Trustworthy Friend

One of the finest friends someone can have is a trustworthy friend. Trust and honesty are the bedrock of every lasting connection. You'll be glad you selected a friend who can be open and honest with you. Even if you don't always feel it now, you'll like it when you reflect on it.

Select a Group of Friends Who Will Challenge You, Inspire You, and Cheer You On

These people also make great purpose partners. Nobody likes a pal who is always down or gloomy. Naturally, we seek those who are uplifting and motivating.

Which social group are your friends a part of? How does your voice sound while you are speaking to them? The best friends will be there to listen sympathetically and help you see the bright side of any situation.

Select Friends That Treat You With the Same Level of Respect You Show Them

The key to a healthy friendship is reciprocal respect. If you want loyal friends, you must first be one yourself.

Additionally, you must inspire, support, and include your friends. Mutual respect and trust are essential components of a successful collaboration.

Pick People Who Will Celebrate Your Accomplishments With You

You want friends who will stand with you rather than just tolerate you. A good friend will acknowledge each milestone, triumph, and accomplishment you encounter. They will be pleased to see you succeed and will congratulate you first. Friends like them are rare, so value them while you can!

Surround Yourself With Go-Getters

Get-it people are dedicated to succeeding and accomplishing their goals. They don't take life for granted or waste their time on pointless pursuits. They take action and finish work effectively. You must surround yourself with people who share your values if you are a get-it person.

Pick People Who Help You Be Your Best Self

Your friends should encourage you to be the most excellent version of yourself. They help you concentrate on finding ways to be true to yourself while pursuing your goals. Your friends should serve as cheerleaders, motivating you to pursue your objectives proudly.

Selecting the right friends to be a part of your inner circle is crucial since they may greatly influence your life. Do they uplift and inspire, or do they bring you down with criticism and negativity? Can you put your faith in them, or do they only harbor resentment because of your success?

Think about the people in your life and what kind of friends you want in the future. Will the people in your inner circle support you through life's ups and downs?

Consider the following as you choose your next friend:

- Just because someone shares your interests and values doesn't mean they're necessarily a good fit for you.
- It's essential to choose friends who make you feel comfortable and accepted for who you are.
- Friendships should be positive relationships where people feel good about themselves and the friendship.
- Do you have similar interests and values?

Along with considering what kind of friends we want, we also need to be aware of the types of friendships we should avoid.

Avoid These Types of Friendships

If you have doubts about a friend, you must consider your instincts. There are warning indications that indicate this person is not a good friend. Perhaps they behave differently in huge crowds or when two or more people are present. Perhaps they only make calls when they have nothing else planned. Here are some warning signals that your friendship might not be ideal:

The User Friend

Some so-called friends desire you when they need you. They developed that friendship out of convenience, and when you've met their needs, they quit acting like friends.

Friends should support one another, but if the support is only given in one direction, it can mean that your friend is using you. These are not positive friendships or partnerships for your future.

Trash-Talking Friends

If your friend is always badmouthing their other friends in front of you, they may be doing the same thing behind your back. If a friend constantly criticizes others, they could be a lousy friend, and you should think again about whether you still want to be in these friendships and connections.

Critical Friend

Friends should support one another, and occasionally, we should correct our friends when they are in error. Good friends might see constructive criticism as a means to improve themselves. In contrast, lousy friends may take offense at being called names.

The Intolerant Friend

Whether in terms of interests, worldviews, or maybe even values, friends will have some disagreements. If a friend constantly criticizes you for what you believe in, then they weren't much of a friend to begin with, were they?

Flaky Friends

It's challenging to maintain a friendship with a flaky friend. They aren't a good friend if you're the type of person who is always trying to get together with friends. They're the type of person who never wants to hang out with you, no matter how much they claim to miss you. Some of your friends might struggle with social anxiety and have trouble making arrangements. Talk to them if it seems they need help to commit to plans. Make it clear that you're not looking to place blame or guilt on your friend but rather to get insight into what may be bothering them.

Invasive Friendships

If your friend becomes upset anytime you are busy with commitments like a job, school, or family, it may indicate a troubled friendship. A good friend is aware of how hectic life may be. If you want to visit your friend, you'll have to wait for a favorable opportunity. These are the relationships that will last a lifetime.

Sexual Friendships

Regular friendships should not be mistaken for sexual friendships or relationships. To be considered a sex friend, you need to connect with another person physically. Still, it's important to note that sex friends are not always close. It is possible to have a close connection with someone you have a sexual friendship with. Still, close and sexual friendships differ, even if they lead to romantic relationships.

Keep the following in mind as you make new friends and say goodbye to the old ones:

- Avoid friendships with people who always bring drama to your life.
- People who are always negative and never have anything good to say.
- Friends who are always busy and never have time for you.
- Friends who take advantage of your kindness.
- Friends who make you feel bad about yourself.

It's normal for friends to argue occasionally, but if yours do so frequently, it might be time to move on.

Consider your pals and decide who you consider a friend, an acquaintance, or maybe a poor friend. Don't be afraid to discuss this openly and honestly with friends to determine whether these relationships are genuine.

CHAPTER 9:

SMALL TALK AND CASUAL INTERACTIONS

We've been there before. You're at a party, a networking event, or even just out running errands, and you find yourself stuck in a conversation with someone you don't know very well. Casual social interactions can be awkward, but they don't have to be.

Principles of Great Conversation

There are ten practical strategies for improving quick conversations and developing the capacity to strike up a conversation at any time.

Show Sincere Interest in the Other Person

A successful discussion depends on having a sincere interest rather than a pretend one. The lack of a driving force will cause the discussion to falter, even if you follow all the guidelines for having a great conversation.

You become socially irresistible when you are curious. Consider how you could respond to the following inquiries when conversing with others:

- What drives this person?
- What matters to them?
- What gives them energy?
- What topics do they like discussing?
- For what reason do they give up hope?
- What do they hold dear?

Make it a point to respond to these inquiries about each individual you deal with to fulfill your social mission. Even if you've been attempting to discover more about the individual, they'll find you interesting before you realize it!

Be genuinely curious about the people you talk to. The point of communicating with another person is to learn more about them.

A few pointers to remember as you converse:

- Pay attention to the person you're talking to. Make eye contact and focus on what they're saying.
- Don't talk too much. Let the other person share their thoughts.
- Be interested in what the other person says. Ask open-ended questions and show that you care.
- Use body language to show that you're engaged in the conversation. Lean in, nod your head, etc.
- Be polite and respectful. Listen more than you talk, don't interrupt, and say thank you when the conversation is over.

With the practical strategies in mind, we will discuss how to master any casual social interactions.

Mastering Casual Social Interactions

All of us have been in circumstances where we were thrown headfirst into a group of strangers and expected to make conversation. Few individuals, including extroverts, like socializing and meeting new people.

Others, however, are comfortable talking to everyone they meet, whether they know them or not. But many people find it challenging to converse with strangers. This might be quite difficult if you suffer from social anxiety disorder (SAD). Even though you struggle with making small talk in social situations, you may work on your communication skills to feel more at ease chatting with new people. Putting in the time to practice is your best bet.

Here are some easy ways to improve your social skills and be friendlier to strangers:

It's a Brief Interaction

First and foremost, remember that whatever social interaction you have (standing in line at a restaurant, on an airplane, etc.) is temporary and will not devour your entire life.

If you remember that, you'll be more likely to pay full attention to every interaction. There is a slim possibility that you will ever encounter some of these individuals again. They will only remember you if you had a good or bad interaction with them. Listen to others; it's the least you can do. It won't last forever.

Shake Hands or Hug

Do not make a gesture that is quite uncomfortable for everyone involved and consists of physically waving toward each other from a distance of five feet. Move toward them in a confident and friendly manner, and present your hand upon introduction. If you shake hands, ensure your handshake has a firm grip and a steady shake.

Joining in on a Discussion

Always make direct eye contact, flash a friendly grin, and offer to start the discussion by introducing yourself before you join in. After that, pay attention and note who else is in the group by name.

How do you recall the names of people? Concentrate, say the name aloud, recall a person with that name, use it in conversation, and repeat it when you finish. Be sure to use their name when you address them in conversation.

Never Discuss Matters That Are Too Private

Almost no information about the other person is known at the outset of such a discussion. Keep the conversation casual by asking about the individual's hobbies, occupation, or immediate environment.

Use Humor to Break the Ice

Simply commenting on the environment you and the other people around you are in is an effective method to discuss with others. Humor would be welcome in this situation.

- In a lecture hall, you may ask your classmate, "Doesn't he look like Harry Potter?"

Never be mean-spirited or judgmental in your remarks; always be positive. You need to put the other person at ease, so they can laugh with you.

- You may follow up your statement about your professor with, "Where's Hedwig?"

It can be challenging to make someone laugh when you don't know them very well. Using humor as a conversation starter can be risky. Nevertheless, a wonderful connection can begin if you meet someone who appreciates comedy like you do.

Always Carry a Smile With You

Last but not least, smile! Most people walk into a room with a frown or no expression because they are afraid of talking to people. So be sure to practice your smile before you walk through the door so that it's ready to spread happiness.

Keep the following in mind as you learn to master causal interactions:

- Smile and make eye contact when meeting someone for the first time.
- Shake their hand with a firm grip.
- Introduce yourself, even if you've met before.
- Use their name during the conversation.
- Be interested in what the other person has to say.
- Don't talk too much about yourself.
- Avoid controversial topics like religion or politics.

Make the good connections you want to make because even if you have to be the one to make the first contact, you'll find that the effort was well worth it. You may have to force yourself to laugh at certain jokes you don't find funny, but you'll brighten someone else's day. Put the phone down, smile, and make some new friends.

The Power of Small Talk

This section will take a look at what small talk is, why we do it, and how you can master any casual conversation that comes your way.

What Is Small Talk, and Why Do We Do It?

The definition of "small talk" is usually accepted as meaningless chatter. We tend to view its use, especially in quick conversations, as superficial or unnecessary. When examined more closely, small talk reveals its true worth and function. Casual conversation serves as an open invitation. It gets people interested and gets the ball rolling for more interaction.

Small talk has several purposes, including defining the connections between coworkers, friends, and new acquaintances (Reddy, 2016).

It helps us define our social connections in a very flexible way by acting as:

Conversation Starter

When two strangers strike up a little conversation, it allows them to realize that the other person is nice and wants to engage in some light conversation. People can develop their reputations and degrees of experience in a professional setting.

However, suppose it is a discussion between two people who are already acquainted. Their small talk is a pleasant icebreaker before moving on to more important subjects. It gives them the ability to gauge the mood of others and express their own mood to build a solid relationship.

Conclusion of the Conversation

An abrupt stop to a conversation increases the chance that the other person will feel rejected. These conversations help lessen rejection, confirm the relationship between two people, and make the parting pleasant.

Filler to Break the Silence

Silences between two individuals are often seen as awkward in most cultures. Phatic discussion can be started until a significant topic comes up to increase comfort. It's because most people find quiet to be uncomfortable at times.

The Benefits of Small Talk

Small talk helps us relax and find our center in the here and now. Many of us frequently experience anxiety or unease when engaging in social interactions. Everyone worries about being rejected, whether they admit it or not.

When we finally muster the courage to speak up about our concerns, these feelings of dread can make us feel physically ill and leave us at a loss for words. Small talk gives us a tool to help us get above these constraints and fears we place on ourselves.

Rather than telling ourselves, "I never know where to start," we could tell ourselves, "What I'll do is say hi and show an interest in someone."

Here are the several benefits of engaging in small talk:

Easy Transitions

Small talk can mark the beginning and end of our days.

We may transition between our many personal or professional roles by engaging in small talk before a medical treatment or beginning a challenging professional endeavor; being able to greet each other in a kind and pleasant way aids in relaxing into the activity or task at hand.

It may ease the tension after a confrontation or dispute and facilitate the transition to a more objective dialogue. It can offer a much-needed break from mounting tensions and unresolved problems. "I know there's more to talk about, but I need a drink. Do you want anything?" A simple conversation can serve as a powerful reminder that it's essential to take breaks back into politeness regularly to maintain goodwill and the possibility of resolving our disagreements in the future.

The Chance to Share

Small talk offers a priceless chance to help, connect, and unite with another individual. When we break the ice with a stranger, we are forced out of our comfort zone and into the company of others. By doing this, we show that we want to connect.

How to Make Small Talk More Interesting

We may remind ourselves that having those uneasy butterflies in our stomachs isn't always a sign of social inability or that we're about to be rejected. Think back to when your stomach flipped before you approached the stranger who turned out to be your closest friend or most loving partner.

Keep the **REACH** method in mind when engaging in small talk:

- **R**eveal yourself. Put on a brave face and introduce yourself to break the ice. "It was mentioned to me by a coworker in the department that this is your first week. I have only been here for a month. How has it gone thus far?"
- **E**xplore the interests of another. "I noticed that your T-shirt was from Greece. Have you visited the area?"
- **A**sk open questions. "I saw an older couple won the lottery last night. If you win, what plans do you have?"
- **C**onsciously listen for information and emotions that someone else could communicate. "You said how eager you are to go home. Where have you been? Have you gone on a business trip?"
- **H**ighlight parallels. "What is your son's age? I have a young child at home who is about his age."

Small talk isn't that insignificant, after all. Allowing small talk to demonstrate its various advantages will enable us to share and enjoy the enormous rewards of kindness and connection. Knowing that we might need a few phrases to become closer to someone at any time gives us hope and encouragement.

Examples of Small Talk Topics and Conversation Starters

Here are a few subjects to consider if you're searching for interesting conversation starters.

Weather

Even though discussing the weather may appear uninteresting, it is a nice, neutral subject that everyone can chat about. Has a severe storm just passed through? Are you now experiencing a heat wave?

Here are some weather prompts:

- This is a beautiful day, don't you agree?
- It appears like there will be rain today.
- I am simply loving this warm weather today!

Next time you're in awkward silence, try one of these weather questions. In the course of the chat, they could bring up other subjects.

Entertainment and the Arts

Conversation-starting themes in the arts and entertainment include:

- Movies and TV programs
- Renowned eateries
- Books
- Music

Some questions you could pose are:

- Do you read any excellent books? I'd appreciate some suggestions.
- Do you have any favorite podcasts?
- Have you recently downloaded any new applications or games you genuinely enjoy?

Remember that small talk aims to establish a connection with the other person. What matters is that you start talking, so be brave and choose any subject you feel confident about!

Sports

Discussions about sports are appropriate topics for someone you don't know well. They may consist of the following:

- Local or neighborhood teams
- Sports activities
- Championships or competitions

You can stay updated on happenings in the world of sports by remembering that American football, cricket, hockey, and golf all have distinct seasons. The Olympics are usually a wonderful choice if they are held since everyone will be talking about them.

Family

People will most likely ask about your family during small talk. You can do the same.

Family-related conversation starters might include:

- Are there any siblings you have?
- When did you start dating your partner?
- Where is the home of your family?

While discussing your family may be a fantastic conversation starter, be careful with any potentially delicate subjects. It may be challenging to ask about someone's plans for having children, for instance, if they struggle with infertility.

Food

If you keep it upbeat and impartial, talking about food may be a terrific topic for small talk. You may inquire about the best nearby eateries, the person's go-to order, or whether they like to cook at home.

- Have you recently tried any new restaurants?

- What is your favorite dish to prepare at home?
- I'm out of creative ideas and am over sandwiches. What are some tasty lunch options for the office?

Keep the discussion upbeat and refrain from going on about meals you don't like, just like with other conversation starters.

Work

Work is a common topic for casual conversations as well. If you like your job, you could be asked what you do. Consider carrying business cards with you at all times, especially if you engage in particular behaviors that are difficult to explain. This works well if your business has a webpage that people can go to for further information.

You may say any of the following in a work-related context:

- How long have you held the position of [insert job title] or worked for the firm [insert]?
- What aspect of your employment do you like the most?
- That kind of work is fascinating. How did you become involved?

Find out from others where they like to go and what they suggest. Many people like lending a hand and are willing to offer their knowledge. Allowing your discussion partner to describe a nice vacation may also be a terrific way to make them feel pleased.

Hobbies

People enjoy discussing their interests, so they'll probably be curious about yours. If you don't currently have any interests, think about finding one. Having a pastime will not only offer you something to chat about, but it will also allow you to meet people who share your interests.

Hometown

You could be questioned about your hometown in casual conversation. Here are some prompts you can ask them in return.

For instance:

- How is your hometown different from where you live now?
- Do you miss your hometown at all?
- How come you left?

Prepare a captivating anecdote or tale if anyone asks you to share more about your hometown experiences. Likewise, ask about the hometowns of others.

Tips for Avoiding Awkward Small Talk Moments

Once you have a few solid conversation starters under your belt, it might be useful to know which types of small talk to steer clear of.

Finances

It's improper to inquire about someone's finances when you've just met them. Asking about someone's job or the positive features of their profession is okay, but avoid asking about their pay. Most individuals would consider this inquiry invasive and inappropriate. If they are experiencing financial hardship, it might make them feel uneasy.

Religion and Politics

When discussing politics, you can never be sure who among your listeners will have strong feelings. Avoid this subject if you don't want to risk being caught up in a heated discussion. Another very private and potentially delicate subject to steer clear of is religion.

Sex

It is improper to bring up sexual topics or pose personal queries in casual chat. When talking to a stranger, don't talk about sexual things directly, and don't make sexual hints. Both are probably going to make people feel uneasy.

Death

Another difficult subject to steer clear of in casual chat is death. Avoid bringing up sensitive subjects that might be distressing while you are with somebody you don't know.

Appearance

If you don't know someone well, avoid asking their age. Even though the query may appear straightforward to you, it might be a confrontational subject for others.

Avoid questions on looks as well. Never comment on someone's weight loss or inquire whether they are pregnant. Because you may never be certain of the cause of weight gain or loss, you can find yourself in an awkward situation.

Health

Health difficulties are typically not good topics for casual chat. The individual with whom you are discussing it might not be as interested in hearing about your current health endeavor or the aches and pains you are experiencing.

Topics to steer clear of or include:

- Advising individuals on how to feel regarding a medical condition.
- Providing "quick fixes" for difficult medical problems.
- Implying that individuals may become in shape or reduce weight by implementing your advice.

Avoid talking about anyone else's or your own possibly delicate health conditions. It's advisable to refrain from inquiring about other people's health since it might come across as invasive.

CHAPTER 10:

DEVELOPING MEANINGFUL FRIENDSHIPS

We all know the saying, "It's not what you know; it's who you know." And while that may be true to some extent, it's also important to remember that it's not just about who you know but also about the quality of those relationships. As we get older, it can become more and more challenging to develop and maintain meaningful friendships. But why is that? And what can we do about it?

Whatever you choose to call it, there are rare moments in everyone's life when they feel an instant connection or commitment to another person that transcends pretty much everything else. These select, unique friendships are unaffected by moves to different places, time spent studying abroad, coming out of the closet, going back in, and coming out again with a wig (because age waits for no one). Few situations may genuinely alter your feelings for one another because of the total acceptance you have for one another.

Some relationships might end due to distance or extended stretches without communication. Another connection can end due to a significant shift in ideals or objectives. However, none of these factors can end an enduring friendship. The bonds between sincere friendships seem to be indestructible.

Some people will never have high-level (intimate) friendships because they only have low-level (surface-level) connections. These individuals fit the definition of "superficial" as a whole. They say hi to everyone, and they know everyone, but nobody knows them well. There is hardly any emotional connection or common past. Furthermore, there is no vulnerability.

Some individuals only maintain close relationships. It's likely that these individuals have a difficult time expressing themselves and are reluctant to venture outside of their comfort zones. And while they have a small number of close friends and family members, they limit their potential by not branching out to meet more people.

The fact is that strong relationships at all levels are essential to our well-being. Just figuring out where everyone fits is the challenge.

What is the good news? Investing as little or as much time as you like in a friend is entirely up to you; if they do the same, your friendship will feel like it will last forever.

Deepen Your Casual Connections

Have you ever attended a work party when everyone you see is someone you know, but neither you nor they truly know well? They are your "coworkers." They are folks you encounter at work—however, some individuals you genuinely like and want to get to know better.

Or perhaps you're new to a town and are trying to connect with people and engage in relationships, but it's been difficult so far. People like to be alone. Being unfamiliar makes it challenging to approach strangers and strike up a conversation. Perhaps you've met a few acquaintances that you occasionally see at happy hours or sporting events. Still, you desire a closer bond and a more genuine friendship with them.

Here are some practical ways to deepen your casual connections:

Be Deliberate and Make Contact

It's critical to approach outreach with purpose. Make your relationships with friends a high priority. A friendship can only develop if you put time and effort into it, just like any other connection. Sometimes we overthink how we appear to others. Do I seem overly eager? Am I being too sincere? Am I scaring them to death? It is okay to express your desire to get out with friends deliberately and explicitly. The individuals you want to invest in will value your intentionality and clarity in leading if they are old enough and open to developing a connection with you. With clear intentions, extend explicit invitations.

Do you want to join us for the basketball game? After work, we're heading to happy hour; would you like to join us? What plans do you have for the weekend? Are you up for a hike? Want to have supper with us?

Laugh Together

Do whatever it is you can with your pal that makes you happy! Doing enjoyable things with a buddy is the most straightforward approach to developing a friendship. Play games, engage in sports, prepare meals, and produce art. Do your favorite activities together. It can be something other than constant face-to-face seriousness and in-depth discussions. Laughter and lightheartedness are healthy for the spirit and for social bonds. Create time in your schedule to be with each other each week, even if that's all it takes to make room for the happiness you contribute to each other's lives.

Listen to Feedback

It's a tremendous compliment to your friend when you seek their input on your choice or your most recent effort. This demonstrates how much you value their opinions if you ask for their advice on improving your self-awareness, forming new routines, and making reasonable adjustments. Good friends give you a fresh perspective on life, regardless of their origins, ideologies, or convictions.

Get Personal

Attend their events, such as birthday parties, baby showers, weddings, and graduation bashes, if you want to maintain excellent relationships. Your presence at significant occasions, even for only an hour, will be cherished and remembered. You can take heartfelt pictures and create enduring memories of a special event and shared experience.

Find or take advantage of opportunities to engage with their significant others, partners, children, valued relatives, and other friends. Learn about their interests and favorite activities to help you develop shared hobbies and passions. Participating in your friends' communities can help you build closer personal ties with them.

Develop Trust

Your friend will more likely create a genuine relationship with you if you encourage them to do the same by disclosing their likes and dislikes, talents and flaws, and achievements and failures. When a friend opens up to you about their personal life, think of it as a step toward developing a genuine relationship rather than a way to gain an advantage, material for gossiping, or social status.

Building trust requires engaging in honesty and openness, maintaining confidence, and demonstrating sincere concern for your friend's well. Follow through on your commitments. If you can't maintain your commitments, renegotiate your terms.

Resolve Conflicts Maturely

Instead of letting animosity linger, communicate your thoughts during confrontations. Instead of arguing to force your friend to agree with you, express your preferences and points of view to promote clarity and communication. Suppose you want to maintain a healthy relationship. In that case, you should avoid utilizing emotional blackmail, including attempts to induce dread, duty, or guilt.

Be a Force for Good

Although having supportive friends might motivate you. You should avoid making continual comparisons that could make you feel inferior or encourage you to outdo others. It's off-putting to make judgments, find fault, or make nasty remarks.

Instead, advocate for your friend's most remarkable traits and most fulfilling experiences. When your friends are talking about their most recent job endeavor or making progress on a creative activity, or if they are generally enthusiastic and motivated, pay attention and share your observations with them. When you remind people of their strengths, and when you are satisfied with your own life, they will appreciate being your friend.

Remember to Value Your Friendships

Refrain from assuming your friendships will always exist. You are taking care of your friendships is essential because, like everything else that's alive, they may wither and die if you don't.

Spend time thinking about your friendships' needs and what they deserve.

A summary of how to deepen your relationships:

- Find something you have in common to bond over.
- Make time for this person in your life, even if it's just once a week or a month.
- Gradually share more information about yourself as the friendship deepens.
- Share something personal about yourself that you haven't shared before.
- Don't be afraid to show them your vulnerabilities.
- Allow them to support you and give you feedback.

Skills in Maintaining a Relationship

Feeling appreciated, encouraged, and part of a community are just some advantages of building genuine friendships. But as you get older, maintaining deep and enduring relationships could be more challenging.

To strengthen your connections with others, try reaching out to them, expressing gratitude, and making yourself emotionally available.

Here is a summary of the most important skills you need to keep in mind as you deepen and maintain your friendships:

- Make time for your friends. Don't always be too busy to hang out.
- Communicate effectively. Let your friends know what's going on in your life and listen to what they say.
- Be understanding and supportive. If a friend is going through a tough time, be there for them.
- Don't gossip or talk behind their back.
- Be positive and upbeat. Nobody wants to be around someone who is always negative

- Keep in touch regularly. Texting, calling, or messaging is better than sporadic contact.
- Show appreciation. Tell your friends how much you appreciate them.
- Set healthy boundaries.

Without clear friendship boundaries, such significant ties may get tense over time. Your relationships may not maintain the essential balance if your boundaries are lacking or if there are none to start with in the first place. But what are boundaries, and how can you set healthy ones? The next section will discuss the importance of boundaries in friendships in more depth.

Establishing Personal Boundaries With Friends

Friends are important. They are the individuals with whom we have trusted, satisfying, and mutually beneficial relationships outside of our families. We receive the love, care, and nurturing we require from our friendships to go through life. They help us remain realistic, focused, and committed to the things that matter most. There is no denying that friends are everything.

You've undoubtedly experienced this yourself: You're at the coffee shop waiting to meet a buddy when they abruptly cancel. Even though it's not the most significant thing in the world, you nevertheless took the time from your day just to meet them, endured traffic to get there, and skipped out on any other prospective arrangements. Although problems arise in everyone's lives, they don't value your time if this friend's behavior is a trend.

What Are Boundaries?

It might be uncomfortable to set limits with friends initially, but doing so is necessary for any friendship to thrive over time. Here, I'll show you how to establish limits in your friendships that are advantageous to both so that you may withstand a lifetime of benefits without eroding through the trying times.

Not only are boundaries an essential part of self-care, but they are also the foundation of any good relationship, including the one you share with your closest friends (Bunch, 2021). Boundaries are frequently established at the beginning of a connection, but occasionally, as the relationship develops, additional boundaries are needed. This is where things get tough since it usually indicates that one buddy requests a change in their current dynamic. Although it's challenging to accomplish, it might be crucial to maintaining one or both partners' mental health.

Why Do We Need to Set Boundaries With Our Friends?

Are you wondering why you would need to set boundaries with your friends?

Here are some common justifications for drawing boundaries with friends:

You Feel Overpowered and Overwhelmed

You can't give from an empty well, and with everything going on in the world and the country, many of us are feeling very depleted. You may say, "I truly wish to be here right now to support you, but I simply don't have the time to be there for you in the manner you deserve." That might spark a discussion about joining a support group, seeing a therapist, or using alternative coping mechanisms than the emotionally draining one-on-one contacts.

In this situation, you may beg your friend to understand that this is just a temporary boundary necessitated by the unusual circumstances of the moment and not a permanent change; in other words, you don't intend to always recommend treatment instead of being a listening ear.

There Is a Change in Your Availability

A friend may sometimes ask for more of you than you are capable of giving or have previously been able to offer, even when everything in the world isn't falling apart. For instance, if you're in a period when other commitments are draining your energy, like having children, you may not be able to provide your friend with the same level of attention and support you did before you had children.

The Connection Is Too One-Sided

When friendships go out of balance, new boundaries often need to be established. It's natural for one person to want to draw the line when putting in far more effort than their friend is, so they don't feel exploited. A mutually beneficial connection is what this kind of boundary is all about.

You Lack Confidence in Sharing

When it comes to the foundations of a relationship, trust boundaries are perhaps the most important. You must have the confidence to share your vulnerabilities with your friend and know that only the people you want to hear what you say will get it. Friendships are often built on this fundamental trust. Still, suppose that trust has been betrayed. In that case, it may be essential to set boundaries on what information you are ready to give or what you anticipate from others when sharing confidential information.

You Can't Stand the Way They Do Politics

This is a hard one since, given the present political atmosphere, some individuals have decided to cut their connections with others who ultimately share their particular political views.

In contrast, if you value the relationship but find it impossible to avoid arguments while discussing politics, you may choose to establish some boundary rules about the subject.

You Don't Like How They Make Fun of You

Friendships may get so intimate that one person might sometimes forget how sensitive the other person is. This could compel you to establish boundaries for taunting or practical jokes about you.

You Communicate Differently

When they are not in a typical setting, not everyone feels at ease speaking in the same way. For example, some individuals could enjoy texting while others would feel more at ease making calls. Whether you fall into the first or second category, it may be wise to establish a boundary if you're feeling overwhelmed by the frequency with which a certain kind of communication is being demanded.

You're Always on Call

You may also need to establish limits on your availability through text or phone. It could make sense to explicitly reset that expectation if you believe that someone expects you to answer the phone or reply right away constantly.

How to Set Effective Boundaries

Without boundaries, friendships may experience tension, disintegration, or even dissolution. Setting appropriate friendship boundaries is crucial for the longevity of any relationship, even if it initially seems strange. Here are the guidelines for establishing boundaries with friends that may help you maintain happy, fulfilling relationships.

Describe How Much You Cherish Your Friendship

It's not about causing wounded emotions when you know how to establish boundaries with friends. In actuality, the reverse is true. Before discussing the subject of boundaries with friends, expressing your appreciation for their friendship is essential. This may help you have a non-confrontational conversation.

Talk With Your Friend

Before enforcing boundaries with friends, explain why you're doing so. Respectfully inform them of your concerns.

Tell them why you believe the boundaries are important, then get their opinion.

Be Specific

When establishing good relationship boundaries, you must be clear about what you expect. Don't be ambiguous. For instance, you can say, "I want you to be a good listener and not speak over me throughout a conversation," as opposed to, "I wish you would listen to me."

You may say, "I want you to quit going in without knocking first," instead of, "Please knock. You are violating my privacy." Being straightforward eliminates any chance for ambiguities that can lead to problems resurfacing in the future.

Be Open to Compromising

Sometimes, you and a friend must acknowledge your differences and find common ground. Perhaps your buddy has a personal limit that is different from yours. For instance, you and your buddy will need to be able to compromise if you like texting while your friend loves video conversations.

Respecting Your Friends' Boundaries

You've attempted to talk a friend out of doing something, but they still ended up doing it. But it's their decision. Your friends should be allowed to make their judgments and errors. You will sometimes agree with your friend's preferences for activities or romantic partners. While having an open discussion about their choices is okay, advising them on what to do is not.

Friendship is about providing support because that person needs to feel capable of taking control of their life. That applies to you as well, of course. When a friend tries to micromanage your life, it's important to let them know that you value their care but can handle major life choices independently.

In every relationship, we must always ask for permission before expressing our opinion or giving advice on another person's choices in life. As a result, before providing advice to a friend, we must determine if they are receptive to it. If we don't, we risk interfering with someone's life too much and maybe causing distance when we truly want to be nearby.

People often claim that since their friend is one of their closest friends and no one else would be as honest as they were, they "had to" tell them what they thought.

Given that you are their closest friends, you must support them in their decision-making process without passing judgment and show them the same respect they deserve. Just remember that if they drew a limit that you may not comprehend, they did so for a purpose and that it is significant to them. As you would want others to respect your boundaries, respect their decisions.

What if the Friend Doesn't Respect Our Boundaries?

How to respond if a friend disregards your specified boundaries:

Describe the Consequences

A boundary is simply a suggestion without a negative outcome.

For instance, if your roommate continues to take your clothing without asking after you've asked them to stop, you might threaten to move out if it occurs again. Reduce defensiveness by phrasing it so they still have an option.

It's crucial to carry out the consequences. Therefore, it makes sense to suggest the ones you'll apply. Verify that it is not only a threat.

Steer Clear of Situations When the Boundary Is Tested

The other person may still not respect your boundaries even after you've done everything in your power to make them explicit. Accept that your friendship may no longer function in specific circumstances or activities if you do not want to end it. Perhaps they prefer to talk while you watch TV, and because you find it annoying, you don't do that activity together.

Think About Ending the Friendship

It's tough to completely change the nature of an established connection, especially if your new limit is a large one. Unfortunately, we risk losing a connection when we create boundaries since every relationship still going strong depends on the present boundaries. Even though it might be painful, the alternative can be to stay in a connection that is no longer beneficial. When you establish boundaries that are beneficial for you, a relationship will last.

CHAPTER 11:

KNOW WHEN TO LET GO

It's perfectly normal to drift apart from some of your friends as time passes. People change and grow in different directions, and that's okay. It's also okay to let go of friendships that have become toxic. Friendship should be enjoyable, not stressful. If you find yourself dreading seeing certain friends or feeling bad after hanging out with them, that's a sign that the friendship might be toxic. If a friendship no longer makes you happy, don't be afraid to let it go.

How to Evaluate Your Friendships and Make Sure They Serve You Well

To maintain a friendship, one must first determine if it is beneficial to their overall well-being or healthy and satisfying. If the latter is the case, one must determine what can be done to turn the friendship around.

The quality of a friendship may be judged by how much it enhances our feeling of self-worth and how much it contributes to our "sense of belonging" (Colino, 2021). When spending time with a specific friend, consider the following inquiries to assess whether your friendship fits this standard:

- Do they invest as much time as I do?
- Can I trust them completely?
- Do I feel understood by this individual, or do they seem to understand where I'm coming from?
- Do they listen to me?
- Do they make me feel good about myself?
- Are they a valued person in my life?
- Do they support my goals and dreams?

If a friendship isn't providing the support you need, you have three options: Confront the problem, let things pass, or distance yourself.

But if you decide to deal with the problem, some consideration beforehand is required. It's essential to gauge the friend's receptivity before attempting to be completely honest about the situation.

Ask yourself:

- What do I want from this if I directly address the issues?
- Do I want to have a back-and-forth discussion about these issues?

If you're struggling to determine whether or not your friend is good for your general well-being and whether you would still like to be friends with them, then it might be time to discuss it with them.

As the first step, acknowledge the relationship between the two of you and make it obvious that you're raising this issue because you place a high value on your relationship. Once you've determined what you want to accomplish and are prepared to discuss it, the second step is to confirm your relationship. Next, concentrate on the connection—everything you find working vs. not working—to get feedback from the other person.

Suppose you encounter any of the following behaviors with your friend, and they are unwilling to try to correct this behavior after you discuss it with them. In that case, it might be time to let go.

Why Do Friendships Just End?

Friendships start and end for the same number of reasons, even in unforeseen, coincidental ways. Like pieces of driftwood carried by the tide, relationships form and fade among people.

We prefer to seek reasonable explanations and logical justifications, yet comprehending relationship disintegration requires acceptance and compassion to better oneself, the other person, and the friendship.

Possible explanations for a sudden breakup in a friendship include:

- Unfair amounts of giving and taking occur inside friendships.
- Disputes or fights arise.
- You outgrow each other.

- External circumstances, such as changing jobs or relocating.

How to Recognize the End of a Friendship

There is no single event that marks the end of a friendship. However, you can notice some indicators that it is about to end (Cox, 2022):

- You begin to communicate less with one another.
- You don't think your friend cares about you.
- You don't enjoy yourselves as much as you used to.
- You no longer behave as yourself around them.
- You have a sneaking suspicion that the friendship is changing.
- Your close friend has a pattern of constantly venting their frustrations to you, which only brings you down.
- Your friend is constantly putting you down and being judgmental of you.
- You feel you put more effort into the connection since there needs to be a proper balance of giving and receiving.
- Your friend doesn't respect your boundaries.

Genuine friendship can be incredibly joyful. However, whether a friendship ends suddenly or gradually, it may leave you depressed and alone. How can you learn to let go of a bad friendship?

What to Do When Friendships Go Bad

It's time to think about reducing the intensity of the connection in some way if you've chosen not to try to mend what's gone wrong. Other options include communicating with that friend less regularly, limiting your interactions with them, or only seeing them in groups. The relationship doesn't necessarily need to be ended, and you are free to leave it open if you choose to do so.

However, if you feel that the friendship has served its purpose and no longer brings you joy, it's perfectly okay to end it. While it's true that some individuals want validation from others before cutting ties with friends, you don't have to wait for things to reach rock bottom before doing so.

Do not resort to "ghosting" a partner after ending your relationship. One option is to openly discuss why the friendship isn't working for you any longer while expressing thanks for the prior information exchanges. A further option is to start a process of separation in which you progressively stop being there and supportive. But suppose the other person still wants to keep the relationship or find closure. In that case, this also necessitates a candid conversation.

There are strategies to get through the grieving process and feel better in the long run. Below are a few ideas:

- **Recognize and Accept Your Feelings:**

  Although getting over a loss might be difficult, closure isn't always possible. It's important to mourn your friendship and give yourself permission to experience your feelings.

  Write them a letter and tear it up if you're having difficulties experiencing your sentiments over your departed pal. As a result, you won't have to be concerned about anybody reading your honest expression of feeling.

- **Put Yourself First:**

  It's simple to place the blame for failed friendships on ourselves. As you make your way through the difficult things, be careful to be kind, especially to yourself. Get in touch with your inner self by meditating, journaling regularly, or spending time in nature.

- **Consult a Mental Health Expert:**

  It may be difficult to cope with the sadness of losing a friend. The feelings and beliefs that might accompany the loss of a friendship can be uncovered by talking with a therapist. You could suppress your emotions if you don't express them. Instead of being digested and metabolized, it doesn't become a part of the way we relate to each other.

In the end, relationships are not set in stone.

Along with friendships changing with time, so may your requirements and understanding of friendship. While it's true that severing ties with an old friend can bring on some regrettable emotions, it can also clear the way for you to focus on strengthening the relationships that truly matter to you.

Here are some things to consider when you decide to end a friendship that no longer serves you:

- Don't feel guilty about prioritizing your time and energy.
- Talk to the other person about what's going on.
- Acknowledge and apologize for your role in the friendship falling apart.
- Don't be afraid to let go of toxic relationships.
- Reflect on what went wrong and what you could have done differently.
- Appreciate the good friends you have.

The Next Step

Friendships are a vital aspect of our lives, but they may end abruptly for a number of reasons, such as a disagreement or a change in circumstances.

There are hints that your friendship could be ending, even if there isn't usually one particular piece of evidence that it has. For instance, you two may not communicate or interact as often as you once did.

Even though it might be difficult to lose a friend, spending more time with friends you already have and developing new ones can be a good beginning in the right direction.

CHAPTER 12:

EMBRACING SOLITUDE

Having strong friendship bonds and embracing your solitude are not mutually exclusive. There's this misconception that to be happy, you need to be surrounded by people constantly. You can't be content unless you're constantly interacting with others and spending every waking moment socializing. But that's just not true. There's nothing wrong with enjoying your own company and being content with solitude; it's healthy! So go ahead and embrace your solitude—it just might be the best thing for you.

Solitude and Loneliness Are Not the Same Thing

The pursuit of solitude is not synonymous with isolating oneself from others. It's all about being in your own company. Finding peace of mind, familiarity with one's thoughts, and the confidence to assert one's identity are all problems with spending time alone.

Although thinking about it might be frightening, it's the only time we spend quality time with our shadow selves (the "depths of the unconscious"), the parts of ourselves that we try to keep hidden (Griffiths, 2017).

The Difference Between Solitude and Loneliness

There is a significant distinction between solitude and loneliness. Loneliness is a depressive condition characterized by a strong feeling of isolation. One gets the impression that something important is missing. The worst kind of loneliness is when you can be with other people yet feel alone.

The state of solitude is being alone but not feeling lonely. It is an optimistic and helpful way to interact with yourself. Being alone in a condition of solitude where you have lovely and ample company is pleasant.

Since humans are, by nature, social beings, they would not be able to fully develop their personalities if they were isolated from other people from the moment they were born. However, as the mental health field continues to develop, we are learning that it is possible to be surrounded by others. In contrast, on the inside, we continue to feel distinct and alone (Griffiths, 2017).

Finding balance is made possible by purposefully setting aside time for solitude. Extroverted people thrive on social interaction, whereas introverted ones can handle loneliness considerably better. Both ultimately require some solitude to achieve peace.

Being alone teaches us that our identities extend beyond the sum total of our responses to our experiences and interactions with others. Instead of a specific physical situation, it's more of a mental state. You may discover solitude by practicing meditation, taking a long walk outdoors, and shutting yourself up for hours with nothing but paper and a pen. Whatever you experience, you'll learn how to assess your life better and view things for what they truly are.

The key points to take away from this section are:

- Solitude is a choice. You can choose to be alone or with others.
- Loneliness is feeling alone, even when people surround you.
- Solitude can be a time of peace and reflection.
- Solitude can help you connect with yourself.
- Solitude is about being content in your own company.
- Loneliness is about wanting to be around other people.

The Power of Solitude: Why You Should Embrace Being Alone Every Once in a While

It isn't a waste of time to arrange a brief period of solitude into your jam-packed calendar. The more hectic your schedule, the more you need peace and quiet.

Numerous studies have praised the advantages of solitude. Here are a few benefits of solitude supported by science (Morin, 2017):

- **Spending Time Alone Develops Empathy:**

  The more time you spend with a select group of people, whether they are friends or coworkers, the more you begin to view the world through a "we versus them" lens. You learn greater empathy for those who might not be in your "inner circle" when you spend time alone.

- **You May Improve and Evolve Your Cognitive Process by Spending Time Alone:**

  The fact is, we are all unique and have had distinct life experiences. No two people are alike in their values, aptitudes, abilities, genetic makeup, and inherent talents.

  This will give you the knowledge necessary to create a style of thinking and a unique way of living that aligns with how you view the world. And using such a strategy will make it easier to discover your life's purpose and goals.

- **Solitude Increases Work Productivity:**

  Studies reveal that being surrounded by others decreases productivity, even though many businesses have begun to design open floor plans to facilitate easier communication (Kim & de Dear, 2013). Having a little privacy while we work helps individuals execute their tasks better.

  Performance does not necessarily equate to production; it just indicates that you completed the task to the required standard. While productivity focuses more on the results or what you get for the hours, money, and effort you put into it, productivity is more concerned with the output.

- **Time Alone Will Support Your Independence:**

  Spending more time alone, taking a few vacations, and participating in enjoyable things you can do yourself all help you grow more independent.

  Your success will always depend on the efforts of those who help you. No one can live by themselves. However, spending time alone engaging in tough tasks that you like will increase your independence if you are someone who finds it difficult to do anything without assistance.

  It will be challenging for someone to realize their potential and increase the value they contribute to society if they are always dependent on others and do not acquire the required life skills.

To become more productive, you must be able to tackle complicated issues independently when the circumstances demand it. Putting in the time to work on yourself without the scrutiny of others can help you gain the independence and self-assurance to take on issues you'll have to confront on your own.

- **Being Alone Inspires Creativity:**

  There's a good reason why a lot of writers or artists like to work in a secluded studio or log cabin. Being by yourself allows your mind to roam, which might spur more creative thinking.

- **You Can Develop Mental Toughness by Being by Yourself:**

  Being social beings, it's critical for us to form lasting relationships with other people. However, solitude could be as significant. According to studies, being able to accept yourself alone is associated with higher levels of pleasure, more life satisfaction, and better stress management. People who value their alone time are less depressed.

- **It Will Give You Perspective on Life's Challenges:**

  We may assess life events more objectively when we step back from everything, block out all the noise and interruptions that distort our thinking, and take a "mental vacation."

  When something terrible occurs to us, we are able to adopt a viewpoint unaffected by the pessimistic ideas that inevitably distort our judgment.

  We acknowledge that everyone has difficulties, but instead of letting them consume us, we attempt to find solutions by considering how we might do better. We develop a greater capacity for gratitude for the good things in our lives.

- **You May Make Plans for Your Future When You're Alone Yourself:**

  Most individuals devote a lot of effort to planning trips and weddings but seldom consider how to maximize their lives. You can check that all of your hustle and bustle has a point when you spend time alone. A quiet setting allows you to reflect on your objectives, achievements, and desired life changes.

- **You Learn More About Yourself in Solitude:**

  You learn to feel more at ease with yourself when you're alone. You can make decisions while you're alone, as there are no extraneous influences or activities, which will enable you to have a deeper understanding of your identity.

Take the Initiative to Schedule Alone Time

Make time to sit quietly and reflect every day, even if it's just for 10 minutes. Turn off all of your devices and give yourself some time to reflect.

It might be uncomfortable at first if you aren't used to being by yourself. To become the best version of yourself, you should carve out that solitary time for yourself.

A quick summary of why alone time is so essential:

- You can focus on your thoughts and feelings without interruption.
- You get to know yourself better.
- You can do what you want when you want.
- You can relax and recharge without feeling guilty.
- You can connect with yourself and your own needs.
- You can learn to enjoy your own company.

How to Find Solitude in a World Full of Noise

Yes, entering the silence by yourself might be a little frightening. When we take a step back and relax, we can finally take stock of our lives and see the details we've been too preoccupied to see before. We may not always feel at ease with what we discover. However, if you have the fortitude to make solitude a daily habit, those trying times will provide you with wisdom that will help you get through difficulties.

But solitude is a practice. To reap the rewards, you must take action. Learning to dance, play golf, use chopsticks, write, use a computer, or write an essay all become simpler with practice. When you can hear what you're thinking and feel what you're feeling, you can completely participate in the present moment, which will make you feel alive again in silence.

How to Begin a Practice of Solitude

Nothing about it is woo-woo. The time you spend alone doesn't have to be punctuated by rituals like praying, chanting, or dancing around a fire. Also, avoid calling it meditation since that would just frighten them. There are just two rules, and they are as follows: Do it alone. Remain silent. The second half is to maintain some degree of stillness. You may access the benefits of solitude in many different ways, such as by going on a walk, gardening in peace, or preparing meals without the distraction of music or the TV. However, it's crucial to stop, be still, and observe.

The following suggestions might also help you find a few peaceful moments during the day:

- **Make It Your Top Priority:**

  Ten minutes a day of quiet time has the same health advantages as taking a shower or brushing your teeth: it will improve your peace of mind. This is a need. It is as crucial to maintaining a healthy body and developing your soul as eating well and exercising.

- **Create a Playlist for "Inner-Working":**

  You can mend and relax by listening to certain music. Include some inspiring podcasts there. While you listen, get some housework done or go outdoors! Our moods are greatly affected by music, which is also known to increase dopamine.

All of these items have the power to improve your mood and help you control your emotions.

- **Vacation in Solitude:**

  We sometimes need to take a break from our hectic lives to refuel. To help you restore your mind and body, consider taking your own vacation. Whether you choose to go nearby or further away, you will be able to spend meaningful time together without the interruptions of daily life.

- **Find Tranquility in Nature:**

  Additionally, it is the ideal location to obtain solitude. Do something relaxing like taking a stroll along the water, going on a solo hike, sitting in a park and people-watching, or just looking up at the sky. For both our physical and emotional well-being, nature is a potent healer.

- **Explain the Value of Quiet Time to Those with You Share a Home With:**

  No music, computers, or television. You should use this time to read, play, or do art yourself. People you live with will start to support and appreciate it if you let them know that it's important to you and set an example for them.

- **Establish at Least One Routine Each Day That Encourages Solitude:**

  Recite a prayer. Spend some time each day in meditation. Do not wear headphones when you run. Before going to sleep, take a lengthy bath or a quick shower. My habit of stillness and coffee in the morning. I make it a habit to get up fifteen minutes earlier on days when I know I'll have a very hectic day ahead of me, simply so that I may sip coffee in peace and quiet.

- **You Can Also Incorporate Solitude Into Your Busy Schedule:**
  - Get away from the city and into nature.
  - Visit a monastery or other religious institution.

- Spend some time with animals; go for a walk in the park with your dog, volunteer at a local animal shelter, or visit a farm.
- Take up a hobby that doesn't involve other people, like painting, gardening, or writing.
- Disconnect from technology and social media for an extended period of time.

Making time for solitude might help you feel renewed and reenergized. Give it high importance. Make room for it. You'll be in a better mood and better able to handle the day's difficulties.

How to Be Content Spending Time Alone

Even if other people might help lift your spirits, there's nothing like being satisfied in your own company. But can you truly be content with yourself?

Yes, but perspective is everything.

You might be able to overcome this loneliness with the appropriate methods.

The greatest manifestation of self-love may be the capacity to appreciate the pleasures of alone time. Not to mention that spending time alone—whether by choice or necessity—allows you to reflect, be creative, or indulge in enjoyable things.

Realize That You Don't Need Anybody Else to Validate Your Value

You don't need anyone else's approval to realize how great you are as a person. Remind yourself that you choose to be alone whenever you find yourself alone. It truly is a decision.

When you set high criteria for the individuals you let into your life, you're telling yourself that you're better off alone than with someone who doesn't fit.

Respect Others' Perspectives, but Prioritize Your Own

If you don't need someone's advice, don't ask. Instead, seek guidance from the inside. What would you do if you already knew the solution to your issue?

That is your responsibility. You start to require less and less counsel from others as you spend more time asking yourself for guidance. When you believe in your ability to overcome difficulties, you grow stronger and more self-assured, taking on tasks you previously wouldn't have believed you could.

Become a Better Observer

If you want to appreciate being by yourself fully, discover unique and unusual ways to see everyday circumstances. Visit a park and see families having fun with their kids or pets. Visit a grocery store and observe how customers purchase their food.

Attempt to comprehend others around you wherever you go. You'll feel closer to people if you understand how they behave when they believe no one is looking.

In a Pitch-Black Space, Close Your Eyes and Enjoy the Stillness

The world is a hectic place, and if you don't give yourself a break from it occasionally, it's easy to overlook how relaxing it can be to just be by yourself and take pleasure in your own company. However, if you take the time to break away from the real world now and then, you won't have this problem.

Sit down for a while in a still, dark space. Tune in to anything that isn't occurring in the immediate vicinity. You may learn a great deal about yourself when you're least busy, so there's nothing to keep you from experiencing the thoughts and sensations you deny yourself throughout your hectic days.

Practice Talking To Yourself

Every individual has an inner voice that communicates with them during all hours of the day and night. Learning who that inner voice is and how to communicate with it is one of the most essential things you can do for yourself.

This voice is easy to ignore when you spend time with others, but when you're alone, it's the only thing keeping you company. You pick up on this voice. It's you. More than anything else, how you communicate with yourself will define you. Practice listening to the inner voice that advocates for you.

Cultivate Hobbies

You're probably too busy with work, family, and regular responsibilities to give any thought to self-care hobbies. Find a new pastime that makes you happy, or return to an old one. Consider engaging in creative endeavors like learning photography or enrolling in a pottery class.

Keep Creating

One of the most significant things you can do in life is create. One of the hardest things in life is creating while everyone (or just one individual) wants your attention.

You are the only person preventing you from producing the art and work you can do alone. The excuses are all over. You may become completely absorbed in your task while you're alone. You know you're making something worthwhile when you become completely absorbed in your task.

Take Yourself on a Date

Learn to perform tasks that society perceives as requiring two people alone. Visit a movie theater by yourself and take in the show. Enjoy a wonderful solo dinner out. Get to know yourself better by going out on dates with yourself.

At first, this will feel uncomfortable. People used to socializing in groups may feel lost when faced with the prospect of spending time alone. Avoid trying to run away from the agony. Embrace it. And then have a good laugh because who thought you couldn't do these tasks yourself?

Furthermore, you must first learn to love these things before you can genuinely enjoy them with others.

Spend Time Giving Back

If you become a hermit when you're alone, look for people you can be alone with. Volunteering your time to an organization you support is a fantastic way to achieve this and make a difference in the world.

Being happy and alone doesn't require isolating yourself from the outside world. It entails having enough self-assurance to realize that others can surround you without relying on them to make you happy.

And a smart place to start is by surrounding yourself with decent people—the types of individuals you'll meet when you volunteer your time for a cause that matters to you.

Embrace your independence, learn to enjoy your own company, seek the things that bring you joy, and treasure the moments you spend by yourself.

Be Your Own Best Friend

Why should I become your best friend? Rather than relying on your significant other, friends, or family members to be with you while you are hurting, it is in your best interest to establish your personal internal support structure. Doing so has a lot of advantages. When your hopes and dreams aren't satisfied by the people in your life, you may experience feelings of disappointment, heartache, and even a complete breakdown of your relationships.

Without turning to others, we all possess the ability to provide for our own needs.

Even if having a strong network of friends and family is fantastic, learning to be more independent is still a good idea. What happens if you don't have anyone to lean on or if they cannot help you when you need it?

Here's how you can become your best friend:

- Make time each day to do something you enjoy (read, take a walk, listen to music).

- Talk positively to yourself in the mirror (tell yourself that you're smart, capable, and loved).
- Be patient when you make a mistake (everyone makes mistakes sometimes).
- Forgive yourself for things that have happened in the past.
- Celebrate your accomplishments, no matter how small they may seem.
- Don't compare yourself to others; focus on being the best version of yourself possible.
- Take care of your body by eating healthy foods and exercising regularly.
- Give yourself permission to relax and enjoy life.

It takes time and effort to develop meaningful relationships with others, just like becoming your best friend. The road to "best friend" status is paved with phone calls, shared calendars, and shared ups and downs. So take the time to get to know yourself and be there for yourself as you would for your friends. The connection you have to yourself is the most significant of all the connections you have.

CONCLUSION

Friends are invaluable. They offer a calming feeling of connection and stability in a chaotic environment. We share our joys and sorrows, laugh and weep together, and give one another support when things are tough. But the voluntary nature of friendship is what makes it special. We are not legally married, related, or financially dependent on each other in any way. This is a very open-ended and unrestricted connection, and we continue to keep it because we choose to.

The drawback of all this flexibility, though, is that friendships frequently lapse due to a lack of formal commitment. Children, spouses, sick parents, and professional commitments that infringe on our personal time may all add to the flood of responsibilities that can make up adult life.

Although making new friends as an adult can be difficult, you now have the tools and knowledge to accept the challenge. This guide provided the necessary tips for making meaningful connections and long-lasting friendships. By following the advice in this guide, you will find friends that will enrich your life.

What did you learn from this guide?

- Why making friends is harder as an adult and how to overcome the obstacles we face.
- That it is never too late to learn to make friends and the reason why friendship plays such an important role in our lives.
- How having friends can improve your mental health and physical well-being.
- The specific and practical social skills you need to make friends and how you can develop your skills to approach anyone in the hopes of making a new friend or for casual conversation.
- Where you can meet new people easily and learn how to approach them.

- You deserve friends who encourage, accept, and support you. And that it's okay to end a friendship if it no longer serves you.
- That you spend time with yourself and become comfortable with being alone in order to grow as an individual.

As you journey down this path of finding meaningful connections with others and making use of the practical advice outlined in this book, you need to remember that the most important friendship you will ever have is the one you cultivate with yourself.

So be kind to yourself; this is a learning curve. Always keep your best interests at heart, use your time wisely, and invest in self-reflection to consider what your needs are.

As the saying goes, you cannot pour from an empty cup! So figure out what you need and what types of friendships will help you prosper, and take the necessary steps to make it happen.

The keyword to take with you on your journey is "action." We must push ourselves outside of our comfort zones in order to grow. Find the people that make you want to be a better person, and because friendships are a mutual give and take if they feel like you help them too, they'll stick around (for a very long time).

Although these steps may seem difficult at first, they will become easier as you practice. Reaching out might make someone's day, and it could be the start of what develops into a long-lasting connection. We benefit so much from having authentic friends; thus, we should put effort and time into cultivating healthy friendships.

It's time to meet new people, embrace the unknown, and cultivate more meaningful connections.

Best of luck to you, my friend.

GLOSSARY

Affect: An emotional experience that a person has that others may identify as their own (Mental Health Literacy, 2022). For instance, if you appear or act depressed, someone else may assume you are depressed.

Affirmation: A declarative statement.

Agreeableness: Appealing to one's senses or mind in a positive way, especially when it meets one's specific preferences or requirements.

Antisocial personality disorder: A specific personality disorder. Individuals who suffer from antisocial personality disorder consistently disregard the rights of others (Mental Health Literacy, 2022). It starts in early adolescence or childhood and lasts till maturity. Sociopath and psychopath are other prevalent names for antisocial personality disorder. Individuals suffering from this personality disorder frequently hurt others without regret or shame.

Anxiety: Anxiety is a distressing physical signal or collection of symptoms (Mental Health Literacy, 2022). Anxiety sufferers endure a range of uncomfortable bodily symptoms tied to anxious thoughts. An anxious person may also worry about things that are unlikely to happen but feel threatened by them. When your anxiety becomes a problem or a condition, it interferes with many aspects of your life, including school, work, pleasure, friends, and family. Anxiety can cause a variety of physical feelings, including but not limited to the following: Concern, ruminations, "butterflies," twitchiness, restlessness, muscular tension, headache, a dry mouth, and the sensation that oxygen is not flowing into the lungs.

Anxiety Disorders: Refer to a spectrum of conditions affecting the mind. People with an anxiety disorder will feel tension in their bodies and minds about their surroundings, be uneasy about the future, and harbor irrational concerns (see anxiety). Anxious disorders are determined by the frequency and severity of the anxiety symptoms and how they affect daily living. Anxiety Disorders include; social anxiety disorder, panic disorders, separation anxiety disorder, and generalized anxiety disorder" (Mental Health Literacy, 2022). Psychological therapy or drugs are both effective ways to manage anxiety disorders.

Body Language: Our gestures, motions, and mannerisms used to interact with others.

Boundaries: Something that establishes or shows a range or limit.

Casual Conversation: An informal or natural exchange between individuals.

Charisma: A unique magnetic allure or appeal.

Communication: A method through which individuals interact by using a shared set of signs, symbols, or actions.

Compassion: Consciousness of the suffering of others and the desire to help them.

Consciousness: The characteristic or state of being aware, specifically regarding something within oneself.

Constructive: Encouraging development or improvement.

Conversation: Oral exchange of thoughts, feelings, observations, or ideas.

Depression: It refers to a mental condition as well as a state of having a low mood. This can be perplexing, as some people experience depression often yet do not suffer from it as a mental condition. Both major depressive disorder and dysthymic disorder can present themselves in people who are depressed. Major depressive disorder (MDD) is a form of depression that affects most people and is considered the most prevalent type of depression (Mental Health Literacy, 2022). In addition to feeling significantly down, sad, depressed, or irritated, someone with MDD also suffers from a lack of interest, diminished enjoyment, despair, exhaustion, sleep issues, appetite loss, and suicidal thoughts. Adverse effects of MDD can be seen in many areas of a person's life, including relationships at home, with family and friends, at work, and at school. Bipolar disorder may also include depression. MDD can be efficiently treated with medicine or psychological therapy.

Development: The ongoing process of growing physically and psychologically (emotionally and cognitively).

Disorder: An irregularity in one's physical or mental condition; disorder is frequently used as a synonym for illness.

Distress: Pain or suffering that affects the body, a body part, or the mind.

Empathy: The process of comprehending, being sensitive to, being aware of, and experiencing another person's feelings, thoughts, and experiences from the past or the present without having those feelings, ideas, or experiences completely stated in an explicitly objective way.

Examine: To carefully evaluate.

Extroversion: This personality type is characterized by someone sociable and outgoing. Those that possess this trait are frequently referred to as "extroverts."

Ghosting: The act or habit of suddenly severing all communication with an individual (such as a former love partner) by refusing to reply to all calls and messages, generally without warning.

Go-Getter: A bold and competitive individual.

Gossip: Rumor or information of a personal nature.

Health: Is not simply the absence of illness or disability; rather, it encompasses a person's mental, social, emotional, and spiritual well-being. That also covers mental health.

Initiative: An initial action.

Intentional: Done on purpose or by design.

Interact: To influence one another.

Interpersonal: Being, referring to, or involving relationships between people.

Introspection: An inward evaluation of one's own feelings and thoughts.

Introversion: Means turning inward, concentrating more on one's internal thoughts than their social environment. People with this personality trait are sometimes referred to as "introverts."

Loneliness: Causing a sense of gloom or despair.

Maintain: To maintain (as of repair, effectiveness, or validity) anything in its current state: protect against failure or decline.

Meditation: The practice or act of contemplation.

Mental Health: Is more than just the absence of mental or behavioral disorders; it is a condition of emotional, behavioral, and social wellness (Mental Health Literacy, 2022). It doesn't imply that you're not in pain. A person might have both mental health issues and mental disorders simultaneously. As an illustration, a person who has undergone successful therapy for major depressive disorder may continue receiving care. They currently experience both mental health and mental illness.

Mental Toughness: The capacity to withstand emotional stress and hardship.

Mindfulness: The art of constantly cultivating a heightened or total consciousness of one's thoughts, feelings, or experiences without passing judgment.

Networking: Sharing knowledge or services between people, groups, or organizations.

Open-Mindedness: The willingness to hear arguments or ideas.

Perception: It is a mental process where information from the five senses—sight, hearing, smell, touch, and taste—is recognized or becomes conscious.

Respect: Having high regard for someone or something.

Self-Awareness: The understanding of one's uniqueness or personality.

Self-Confidence: Assurance regarding one's individuality, commitment, and capabilities.

Self-Esteem: A sense of confidence and contentment in oneself.

Social: Means being able to communicate and socialize in manners that others understand and are suitable for the context and culture in which you find yourself.

Social Anxiety Disorder: Also referred to as "social phobia," it is a condition where a person has anxiety when required to interact with others (Mental Health Literacy, 2022). Those with social anxiety disorder likewise avoid the circumstances that make a person feel anxious. Public speaking, performing, and partying are examples of fears. Psychotherapy or medication are both effective treatments for social anxiety disorder.

Solitude: Separation from or isolation from the rest of society.

Values: Worth, usefulness, or significance in comparison to anything else.

Visualize: To perceive something visually or to conjure up an image of it in one's mind.

REFERENCES

Arnold, T. (2019, January 8). *10 tips on mastering awkward social situations.* The Tary Arnold. https://www.thetarynarnold.com/blog/being-less-awkward

Beau, A. (2018, October 8). *How to Deepen—Not Just Maintain—Your Friendships.* Shine. https://advice.theshineapp.com/articles/how-to-deepen-not-just-maintain-your-friendships/

Bedsworth, J. (2022, May 20). H*ere Are 9 Ways to Make Friends as an Adult.* GoodRx. https://www.goodrx.com/health-topic/mental-health/how-to-make-friends-as-an-adult

Bernz, J. (2022, June 2). *How Embracing Solitude Helps Me To Become More Productive.* The Good Men Project. https://goodmenproject.com/featured-content/how-embracing-solitude-helps-me-to-become-more-productive/

Bockarova, M. (2021, March 28). *Making Adult Friends Is Hard: Here Are 40 Reasons Why.* Psychology Today. https://www.psychologytoday.com/za/blog/romantically-attached/202103/making-adult-friends-is-hard-here-are-40-reasons-why

Bongers, A., & Macartney, D. (2020, September 8). *Conversation.* Pressbooks.pub; Pressbooks. https://ecampusontario.pressbooks.pub/scientificcommunication/chapter/conversation/

Brown, T. (2020, May 4). *10 Principles for Good Dialogue.* Medium. https://medium.com/practicing-politics/10-principles-for-good-dialogue-c5a11a5b8f29

Bunch, E. (2021, January 20). *How to Set Healthy Friendship Boundaries.* Well and Good. https://www.wellandgood.com/how-set-healthy-boundaries-with-friends/

Cabane, O. F. (2013). *The charisma myth : how anyone can master the art and science of personal magnetism.* Penguin.

Campbell, P. (2013). *5 Ways to Find Quiet in a Chaotic Day.* Psychology Today. https://www.psychologytoday.com/us/blog/

imperfect-spirituality/201312/5-ways-find-quiet-in-chaotic-day

Celes. (2021, April 17). *10 Rules of a Great Conversationalist.* Personal Excellence. https://personalexcellence.co/blog/conversation/

Charisma. (2020). ScienceDaily. https://www.sciencedaily.com/terms/charisma.htm

Chef, K. (2022, July 15). *How to Be Happy Alone - 10 Tips on How to Spend Time Alone.* Today. https://www.today.com/life/inspiration/how-to-be-happy-alone-rcna33959

Christian, K. (2021, March 25). *What Does It Mean To Be A Good Friend?* The Good Trade. https://www.thegoodtrade.com/features/how-to-be-a-good-friend

Chukwuemeka, S. (2022, October 4). *How To Choose The Right Friends: 10 Wise Tips.* Bscholarly. https://bscholarly.com/how-to-choose-the-right-friends/

Colino, S. (2021, November 22). *The friendship checkup: How to reevaluate relationships and take steps to repair them.* The Washington Post. https://www.washingtonpost.com/lifestyle/2021/11/22/reevaluate-friendship-repair-toxic-conversation/

Cooks-Campbell, A. (2022, May 15). *How to Improve Social Skills: 10 Tips to Be More Social.* Better Up. https://www.betterup.com/blog/how-to-improve-social-skills

Coskun, A. (2016). *Interpersonal problem solving, self-compassion and personality traits in university students.* Educational Research and Reviews, 11(7), 474–481. https://doi.org/10.5897/err2015.2605

Cox, J. (2022, July 14). *How To Cope With a Friendship Suddenly Ending*. Psych Central. https://psychcentral.com/relationships/how-to-cope-with-a-friendship-suddenly-ending#how-to-cope

Cunic, A. (2021). *I Have No Friends: Here's What to Do.* Verywell Mind. https://www.verywellmind.com/i-have-no-friends-what-to-do-5200867

Cunic, A. (2022, March 22). *How to Talk to a Stranger.* Verywell Mind. https://www.verywellmind.com/how-to-start-a-conversation-with-a-stranger-3024391

Dr. Mark Ellison. (2020, January 23). *Discovering silence, solitude and night darkness in a world full of everything else.* Hiking Research. https://hikingresearch.wordpress.com/2020/01/22/discovering-silence-solitude-and-night-darkness-in-a-world-full-of-everything-else/

Epstein, S. (2022, February 15). *8 Destructive Beliefs About Friendship.* Psychology Today. https://www.psychologytoday.com/us/blog/between-the-generations/202202/8-destructive-beliefs-about-friendship

Four Reasons Friendship Is Important for Adults. (2022, March 28). Urban Wellness. https://urbanwellnesscounseling.com/4-reasons-friendship-is-important-for-adults/

Fiske, S. T., Cuddy, A. J. C., & Glick, P. (2007). *Universal dimensions of social cognition: warmth and competence.* Trends in Cognitive Sciences, 11(2), 77–83. https://doi.org/10.1016/j.tics.2006.11.005

Gombas, L. (2022, April 19). *The Difference Between Solitude & Loneliness.* Coach Training EDU. https://www.coachtrainingedu.com/blog/solitude-vs-loneliness//

Goodlet, N. (2014, October 21). *5 Ways to Become Your Own Best Friend.* Lifehack. https://www.lifehack.org/articles/lifestyle/5-ways-become-your-own-best-friend.html

Gordon, S. (2019). *How to Make Friends as an Adult.* Verywell Mind. https://www.verywellmind.com/how-to-make-friends-as-an-adult-4769076

Griffiths, D. (2017, December 13). *What's the Difference Between Solitude and Loneliness?* Psychreg. https://www.psychreg.org/what-difference-between-solitude-loneliness/

Gupta, S. (2021). *Why Can't I Make Friends?* Verywell Mind. https://www.verywellmind.com/why-can-t-i-make-friends-5199203

Höpfner, J., & Keith, N. (2021). *Goal Missed, Self Hit: Goal-Setting, Goal-Failure, and Their Affective, Motivational, and Behavioral Consequences.* Frontiers in Psychology, 12. https://doi.org/10.3389/fpsyg.2021.704790

How to Be Charismatic: The Science and Strategies of Likability. (2020, December 22). Healthline https://www.healthline.com/health/how-to-be-charismatic#takeaway

Instant Charisma Formula (Presence + Power + Warmth). (2019, January 15). Salesman.org. https://www.salesman.org/the-instant-charisma-formula-presence-power-warmth/

Kalkhoff, W., Thye, S. R., & Gregory, S. W. (2011). *Nonverbal Vocal Adaptation and Audience Perceptions of Dominance and Prestige.* Social Psychology Quarterly. https://journals.sagepub.com/doi/abs/10.1177/0190272517738215

Kim, J., & de Dear, R. (2013). *Workspace satisfaction: The privacy-communication trade-off in open-plan offices.* Journal of Environmental Psychology, 36, 18–26. https://doi.org/10.1016/j.jenvp.2013.06.007

Konrath, S. H., O'Brien, E. H., & Hsing, C. (2017). *Changes in Dispositional Empathy in American College Students Over Time: A Meta-Analysis.* Personality and Social Psychology Review. https://journals.sagepub.com/doi/10.1177/1088868310377395

Lancia, G. (2021, May 21). Social Skills Training for Adults: 10 Best Activities + PDF. PositivePsychology.com. https://positivepsychology.com/social-skills-training/

Lemola, S., Räikkönen, K., Gomez, V., & Allemand, M. (2012). *Optimism and Self-Esteem Are Related to Sleep. Results from a Large Community-Based Sample.* International Journal of Behavioral Medicine, 20(4), 567–571. https://doi.org/10.1007/s12529-012-9272-z

Lizzie. (2021, October 6). *What Is the Difference Between Work Performance and Productivity?* Make Your Biz Fizz. https://makeyourbizfizz.co.uk/2021/10/06/what-is-the-difference-between-work-performance-and-productivity/#:~:-text=Performance%20only%20means%20that%20you,you've%20put%20into%20it.

Lusinski, N., & Gagliano, S. (2018, June 11). *9 Boundaries You Should Have In Your Friendships, According To Experts.* Bustle. https://www.bustle.com/life/9-boundaries-you-should-have-in-your-friendships-according-to-experts-9345200

Making Good Friends. (2021). Help Guide. https://www.helpguide.org/articles/relationships-communication/making-good-friends.htm#:~:text=Friends%20bring%20more%20happiness%20into,impact%20on%20your%20physical%20health

Manson, M. (2017, February 10). *What Real Friends Look Like.* Mark Manson. https://markmanson.net/what-real-friends-look-like

Mental Health Literacy. (2022). Https://Mentalhealthliteracy.org/Schoolmhl/Wp-Content/Uploads/2018/02/Mental-Health-Glossary.pdf; Mental Health Literacy. https://mentalhealthliteracy.org/schoolmhl/wp-content/uploads/2018/02/mental-health-glossary

Miller, L. (2021, February 23). *11 Qualities Of A Good Friend & Ways To Be An Even Better One.* Mindbodygreen.com. https://www.mindbodygreen.com/articles/how-to-be-a-good-friend

Morgan, N. (2014, December 11). *Which Makes A Better Speaking Voice - High Or Low?* Forbes. https://www.forbes.com/sites/nickmorgan/2014/12/11/which-makes-a-better-speaking-voice-high-or-low/?sh=6f9df59d3905

Morin, A. (2018). *How to Be More Confident: 9 Tips That Work.* Verywell Mind. https://www.verywellmind.com/how-to-boost-your-self-confidence-4163098

Morin, A. (2022, October 12). *7 Science-Backed Reasons You Should Spend More Time Alone.* Forbes. https://www.forbes.com/sites/amymorin/2017/08/05/7-science-backed-reasons-you-should-spend-more-time-alone/?sh=467d64ae1b7e

Murphy, B. (2021). *9 Simple Habits That Will Improve Your Emotional Intelligence.* Inc.Africa. https://incafrica.com/article/bill-murphy-jr-9-simple-habits-that-will-improve-your-emotional-intelligence

Nimmo, K. (2019, October 22). *8 Ways To Be More Charismatic (But Still Be Yourself).* Medium; On The Couch. https://medium.com/on-the-couch/8-ways-to-be-more-charismatic-but-still-be-yourself-408c3e1baf0

Patterson, R. (2020, January 23). *10 Ways to Improve Your Social Skills and Be More Outgoing.* College Info Geek. https://collegeinfogeek.com/social-skills/

Rafiei, H., Senmar, M., Mostafeie, M. R., Goli, Z., Avanaski, S. N., & Mafi, M. H. (2018, November 20). *Self-confidence and attitude of acute care nurses to the presence of family members during resuscitation.* British Journal of Nursing. https://www.magonlinelibrary.com/doi/abs/10.12968/bjon.2018.27.21.1246

Ranaivoson, J. (2022, March 9). *Cultivating Deeper Friendships.* Family Fire. https://familyfire.com/articles/cultivating-deeper-friendships

Ravenscraft, E. (2020, January 23). *An Adult's Guide to Social Skills, for Those Who Were Never Taught.* The New York Times. https://www.nytimes.com/2020/01/23/smarter-living/adults-guide-to-social-skills.html

Raypole, C. (2020, August 17). *6 Ways Friendship Is Good for Your Health.* Healthline; Healthline Media. https://www.healthline.com/health/benefits-of-friendship

Reddy, C. (2016, April 26). *Small Talk - Importance, Benefits, Purpose and Tips.* Wisestep. https://content.wisestep.com/small-talk-importance-benefits-purpose/

Regan, S. (2020). *20 Simple Ways To Make Friends As An Adult, Recommended By Experts.* Mindbodygreen.com. https://www.mindbodygreen.com/articles/how-to-make-friends-as-an-adult

Schawbel, D. (2012, April 15). *How to Master the Art and Science of Charisma.* Forbes. https://www.forbes.com/sites/danschawbel/2012/04/13/how-to-master-the-art-and-science-of-charisma/?sh=2dc2a31c3b47

Self-Care Tips for the Body & Soul. (n.d.). Duke University Personal Assistance Service. https://pas.duke.edu/concerns/well-being/self-care-tips

Simon, O. (2021, April 29). *Presence, Power, Warmth: 3 Steps to Developing Charisma.* Life Intelligence. https://www.lifeintelligence.io/blog/presence-power-warmth-3-steps-to-developing-charisma

Smith, K. (2022, February 4). *How to Set Healthy Boundaries With Friends.* Talkspace. https://www.talkspace.com/blog/friendship-boundaries/

Stanley, A. (2018, February). *21 Best Ways to Meet New Friends in a New City or Town.* MAS Medical Staffing. https://www.masmedicalstaffing.com/blog/best-ways-to-meet-new-friends-in-a-new-city/

Social Value of Small Talk. (2016, March 4). HuffPost. https://www.huffpost.com/entry/the-social-value-of-small-talk_b_9319842

Tamir, D., & Mitchell, J. P. (2012, May 7). *Disclosing information about the self is intrinsically rewarding.* ResearchGate; National Academy of Sciences. https://www.researchgate.net/publication/224919007_Disclosing_information_about_the_self_is_intrinsically_rewarding

Tervooren, T. (2012, May 23). *13 Rules for Being Alone and Being Happy About It.* Riskology. https://www.riskology.co/alone/

Thorp, T. (2016, August 5). *Charisma: 7 Ways to Improve Your Communication with Body Language.* Chopra; Chopra.

https://chopra.com/articles/charisma-7-ways-to-improve-your-communication-with-body-language

Tsai, C.-L., Chaichanasakul, A., Zhao, R., Flores, L. Y., & Lopez, S. J. (2014). *Development and Validation of the Strengths Self-Efficacy Scale (SSES).* Journal of Career Assessment. https://journals.sagepub.com/doi/10.1177/1069072713493761#tab-contributors

Vrabel, J. K., Zeigler-Hill, V., & Southard, A. C. (2018). *Self-esteem and envy: Is state self-esteem instability associated with the benign and malicious forms of envy?* Personality and Individual Differences, 123, 100–104. https://doi.org/10.1016/j.paid.2017.11.001

What Is Friendship? (2018, May 7). BetterHelp. https://www.betterhelp.com/advice/friendship/define-friend-a-good-understanding-of-the-friend-definition/

What is Self-Confidence? (2022). University of South Florida. https://www.usf.edu/student-affairs/counseling-center/top-concerns/what-is-self-confidence.aspx

Whelan, C. (2019, July 11). *12 Simple Ways to Make Friends as an Adult.* Reader's Digest; Reader's Digest. https://www.rd.com/list/how-to-make-friends-as-an-adult/

Williams, D. (2015, March 13). *10 Tips to Help You Keep More Good Friends.* Lifehack. https://www.lifehack.org/articles/communication/10-tips-help-you-keep-more-good-friends.html

Winn, L. (2020, March 16). *Feeling Lonely? 4 Questions To Help Build Authentic Friendships.* Sass Magazine. https://sassmagazine.com/strong-friendships/

Woodman, T., Akehurst, S., Hardy, L., & Beattie, S. (2010). *Self-confidence and performance: A little self-doubt helps.* Psychology of Sport and Exercise, 11(6), 467–470. https://doi.org/10.1016/j.psychsport.2010.05.009

Yankovich, G. (2022, August 23). *How to Make Friends as an Adult, According to Experts.* SELF; SELF. https://www.self.com/story/how-to-make-friends-as-adult

Ybarra, O., Burnstein, E., Piotr Winkielman, & Rodriguez, J. (2008, March). *Mental Exercising Through Simple Socializing: Social Interaction Promotes General Cognitive Functioning.* ResearchGate; SAGE Publications. https://www.researchgate.net/publication/5640069_Mental_Exercising_Through_Simple_Socializing_Social_Interaction_Promotes_General_Cognitive_Functioning

Young Entrepreneur Council (YEC). (2017, March 28). *10 Ways to Become a More Charismatic Person.* Success. https://www.success.com/10-ways-to-become-a-more-charismatic-person/

Quote from The Alchemist. (2022). Goodreads.com. https://www.goodreads.com/quotes/11195-when-we-love-we-always-strive-to-become-better-than

Made in the USA
Las Vegas, NV
03 January 2024

83834182R00083